HATCHING: PIRANESI & TAFURI

VICTORIA WATSON

An AIR Grid Publication

ISBN: 97809928768-8-3

INTRODUCTION

This book presents an interpretation and a critical design proposal, it was inspired by Manfredo Tafuri's essay The Wicked Architect: G.B. Piranesi, Heterotopia and the Voyage. Tafuri's essay was published as the Introductory chapter to his book *The Sphere and the Labyrinth, Avant-Gardes and Architecture from Piranesi to the 1970s.*

The book is organised as a kind of journey that travels between Tafuri's writing about Piranesi and the design of a one kilometre long housing block, known as Corviale that was built in the 1970s on the southwestern periphery of Rome.

Hatching: Piranesi & Tafuri is a re-working of an earlier publication of the same title, published in 2015 by the Big Air World. It is a supplement to *Utopian Adventure: The Corviale Void*, which was published in 2012 and suported by a scholarship from the British School at Rome, awarded to the author in 2010.

PART ONE

One is led almost automatically to the discovery of what may well be the 'drama' of architecture today: that is to see architecture obliged to return to pure architecture, to form without utopia; in the best cases to sublime uselessness.[1]

Manfredo Tafuri, 'Architecture & Utopia'

The Invention, fixed and circulated by means of the etching, renders concrete the role of utopia, which is to present an alternative that departs from actual historical conditions, one that pretends to be in a meta-historical dimension, but only in order to project into the future the bursting forth of present conditions.[2]

Manfredo Tafuri, 'The Wicked Architect'

Some three years after arriving in Rome, the architect, Giambattista Piranesi, produced his first independent publication, the *Prima parte di architetture, e prospettive*, of 1743.[3] It included a suite of twelve etchings (increased to 16 in subsequent editions)[4] that showed fantastic views of an imaginary city. The built forms shown in the views could be read as hypothetical projections of an imaginary architectural language, one that appeared to have been derived from the remains of antiquity that lay scattered around the city (figure 1). As well as the views the Prima parte included a written dedication, addressed to one of Piranesi's patrons, a Venetian builder named Nicola Giobbe, Piranesi wrote:

I will not tire you by telling you once again of the wonder I felt in observing the Roman buildings up close, of the absolute perfection of their architectonic parts, the rarity and the immeasurable quantity of the marble to be found on all sides, or that vast space, once occupied by the Circuses, the Forums and the Imperial Palaces: I will tell you only that those living, speaking ruins filled my spirit with images such as even the masterfully wrought drawings of the immortal Palladio, which I kept before me at all times, could not arouse in me. It is thus that the idea has come to me to tell the world of some of these buildings.[5]

Reflecting on the conditions of architecture in the late 1970s, the architectural historian and critic, Manfredo Tafuri, was drawn to Piranesi's dedication. He saw in it the key parameters of a psychodynamic system called 'utopia.' It interested Tafuri because he thought he could use it to remind contemporary architects about the relationship between modern architecture and utopia. Through his reading of Piranesi, Tafuri was able to identify four key parameters of utopia.

First, utopia involves desires, triggered through direct experience of built form, which so move the subject

Figure 1

Giambattista Piranesi, Prima parte di architetture, e prospettive, first published in Rome, 1743, four views

they find themself compelled to invent new forms. Second, economic and political circumstances mean that drawing is by far the most practical and effective means for making the newly imagined forms publicly known. Here is Piranesi explaining why:

The truth is that today we see no buildings as costly as, for example, a Forum of Nerva, an Ampitheatre of Vespasian, a Palace of Nero; nor have Princes or private citizens appeared to create any; no other option is left to me, or to any other modern Architect, than to explain his own ideas through drawings and in this way to take away from Sculpture and Painting the advantage that, as the great Juvarra said, they have in this respect over Architecture; and to take it away as well from the abuse of those who possess wealth, and who make us believe that they themselves are able to control the operations of Architecture.[6]

The third parameter is revealed in this same quotation. Notice how Piranesi justified his need to draw by alluding to something that is lost - the splendour of ancient Roman architecture - and his commitment to exploring and exposing that loss.

The fourth parameter relates to time, it is perhaps the most difficult to grasp. Piranesi argued his proposals for new forms were, simultaneously, valid for the future, as buildings to be realised and, for the present, as forms that critiqued the conditions of urban and architectural patronage influencing building in Rome in his day. The logical implication of utopia's temporal dimension is that the proposed forms, should they ever be realised, must inevitably provoke disappointment. Because, by the fact of their realisation, the propositional dimension of the forms is lost and they become simply new buildings in the here and now. As such, the forms are no longer able to evoke those feelings of anticipation that made them seem so exciting as projects on paper.

The Campo Marzio

In 1762, nineteen years after the Prima parte, under the title *Campo Marzio della Roma antica,*[7] Piranesi published his project for the development of the Campo Marzio area in the centre of Rome. Tafuri explains how this project enabled Piranesi to take his utopian thinking much further. The centre piece of the Campo Marzio is a six plate ensemble, an enormous engraved plan projection measuring 1350 x 1170 mm in total (figure 2). The grandiose title block, in the top left hand corner, announces in bold letters: Ichnographiam Campi Martii Antique Urbis. The plan represents a portion of Rome, stretched out along the Tiber and bounded to the southwest by the Tiberina island and to the northeast by the Milvian bridge.

The composition of the Ichnographiam is striking, it depicts a large field packed-full of the plans of buildings.

Figure 2

Giambattista Piranesi, Ichnographiam Campi Martii antiquae urbis, formed of six prineted copperplates, together measuring 1350mm x 1170mm

Each plan is formed from a multitude of spatial cells and these are joined by means of radial and bilateral symmetries. Within any one particular plan, adjacent cells appear to be fused together, as if their forms had been generated by a process of gemmation, the one having popped-out of the other, like a bud on a plant. On the other hand, the spaces between the building plans appear to be without order, so the individual buildings appear to be bound to one another by nothing more than the fact of their being packed together in the same spatial field (figure 3). To use Tafuri's words, the Campo looks like *'a formless heap of fragments colliding, one against the other,'* and in so doing, taking on *'the appearance of a homogeneous magnetic field jammed with objects having nothing to do with each other.'* [9]

Tafuri read the Campo Marzio, not as the invention of a new urban and architectural system but as *'an active decomposition*' of an old one.[10] According to him, by exploring the formal possibilities of architecture in dissolution, Piranesi had exposed the arbitrary nature of the presupposed rules of architectural composition and in so doing, raised questions about the communicative function of architecture. As already mentioned, Tafuri's reading of Piranesi was produced in the 1970s, for him a time of crisis in architecture. Tafuri elected to study Piranesi because he thought his work exemplified a similarly critical historical moment in the history of architecture.

Tafuri used Piranesi to deduce general principles, or performative strategies, which, he suggested, might be deployed as a means for dealing with architecture's contemporary condition of crisis. Tafuri's principles suggest architecture in crisis i) needs to learn how to work with degraded materials, ii) must learn how to work in silence, iii) must learn to use publicity as a means of attracting attention.

With these principles in mind we return to the Campo Marzio to interface Tafuri's ideas with Piranesi's presentation of his project.

Although the Ichnographiam is the centre piece of the Campo Marzio it does not stand alone but is supported by a whole series of supplementary plan projections. These are grouped around specific themes and montaged together on single sheets, all of them that is except one. The exception is the Topographia Campi Martii, a single drawing occupying a single sheet. Because of its singularity, the Topographia carries greater significance than all the other supplementary plans (figure 4). It is a map of the Campo Marzio area and the surrounding environs, showing the geographical features of the territory, including the characteristic bending of the Tiber and the encroaching hills that define it.

The Topographia also shows the key roads and

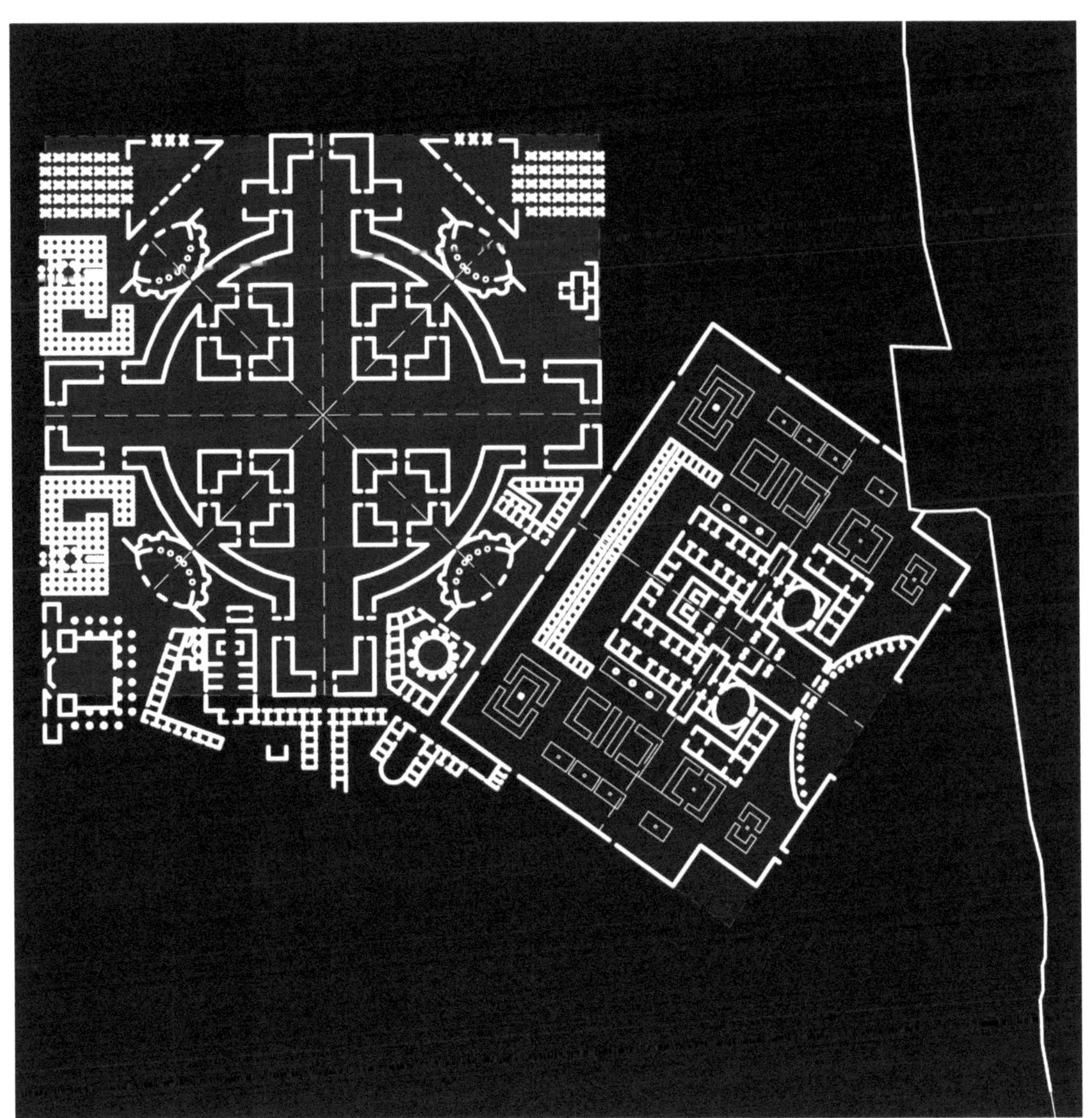

Figure 3

Detail traced from the Ichnographiam Campi Martii showing forms colliding against one another and becoing chipped, like fragments of broken pottery

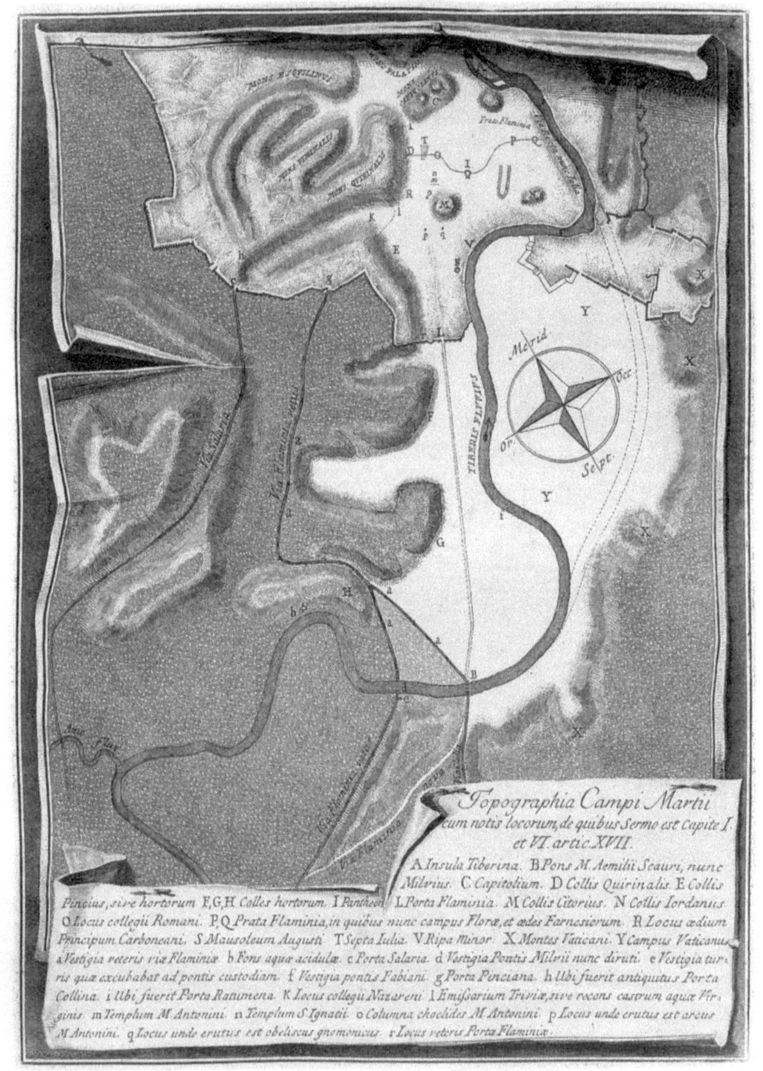

Figure 4

Giambattista Piranesi, Topographia Campi Martii, a single printed copperplate measuring 385mm x 275mm

monuments of the ancient Roman city, such as the Via Flaminia, the Pantheon, the Mausoleum of Augustus, the Circus Agonalis. These all appear as tiny plan footprints, abstractions of their ruined form. The Topographia compliments the Ichnographiam by showing the Campo Marzio area as if stripped-bare of all Piranesi's imaginary forms; but it also shows the area stripped-bare of the buildings that actually were there at the time Piranesi was working on his project.

The mental act of stripping-bare, necessary to conceive the Topographia, involves the same temporal structure, introduced above, that is a necessary parameter of utopia. The building plans packed into the Campo Marzio are not utopian per se, but they become utopian because they pretend to replace an actual urban formation, the one that Piranesi had removed in order to draw the Topographia.[11]

Turning to another drawing in the Campo Marzio set, the Scenographia Campi Martii, which shows the prepared ground of the Topographia in 'birds-eye' perspective (figure 5). Here the ground appears as a bare landscape, stripped of all building, except for the tiny carcasses of the ancient Roman monuments. The scenographic view into the Campo is framed by a collection of antique fragments, drawn in elevation but given depth by their oblique projection, back into the picture plane. The fragments look like they are perched on a ledge, looking down into the Campo.

The relationship between the Campo and the fragments is ambiguous. It is not at all clear if the fragments have been removed from the Campo, or if they are waiting to be allocated a place down there. What is more, the viewer seems to belong to the same temporal dimension as the fragments, as if they too have been removed from their proper place and are suspended, temporarily set aside in some other place.

Gazing into the Scenographia is magical and disturbing at the same time. Magical, because it is like looking from the outside into some other world, disturbing, because that world, for all its remoteness, seems strangely familiar.

Although rarely as explicit as Piranesi rendered it here, in utopian imagining there is always a curious mixture of magic and disturbance.

Figure 5

Giambattista Piranesi, Scenographia Campi Martii, a single printed copperplate measuring 490mm x 730mm

PART TWO

At the same time Tafuri was writing about the Campo Marzio, the Italian Istituto Autonomo per le Case Populari (IACP) was sponsoring a number of housing projects for the outskirts of Rome. The initiative was prompted by the 1962 regional plan that, amongst other things, aimed to alleviate crowding in the city. One project was a residential complex known as Corviale; it was designed in the years 1972-1974, with building work beginning in 1975 and ending in 1982.[12] Corviale is in the southwestern sector of the city and to this day remains very much on the edge, where it is surrounded by farmland.

Since the day people began to move in, Corviale was regarded as a species of architectural *failure* - failure because the inspired civic ambitions of the project were never realised. Corviale provided housing for 8,000 people, but it was supposed to do more than that. It was supposed to provide the infra-structure, necessary to function as a micro-city, a place where people could live together as a civic community. Conceived as a small city and not just an aggregate of dwelling units, Corviale was intended to provide civic and social buildings and places. Some of these were realised, but most were not.

What was especially disappointing about Corviale and remains problematic to this day, was the failure to provide good public transport. Not only is Corviale poorly linked to the centre of Rome but it is isolated from the entire metropolitan region.

Formerly, what is striking about Corviale, the dominant feature of the realised development, is a single, linear, housing block, one kilometre long (figure 6), with a monumental void space inside. The void is open to the sky and stretches along the entire length of the block. The block is punctuated by a number of vertical towers, serving as entry points and means of circulation. But the towers hardly disturb the monumental singularity of the void, they are little more than local incidents along its length. This is because the void is dominated by an underlying order that draws the block and all its incidental details together, into a systematic construct.

The block is formed out of a single figure, a cross-wall, replicated at six metre intervals and made to march, for one kilometre, down the entire length. The shape and organisation of the cross-wall assembly holds the void within the block, where it presents a space that is both accessible and remote. Residents and visitors to Corviale can look into the void, they can walk around it on balconies, but there is no possibility of standing inside. At ground floor level the void is sealed-off from the rest of the building by high concrete walls (figure 7, right).

Figure 6

Exterior views of the one kilometer long housing block that dominates the Corviale development

Figure 7

Two views into the Corviale void. Left, looking up, right, looking down - note the concrete walls that seal off the void at ground level

Gazing into the void is like gazing into Piranesi's Scenographia Campi Martii, it combines magic and disturbance. The viewer looks into the bleak world of the void, it is a strangely familiar experience, like looking down from a local footbridge onto the receeding lines of a railtrack below.

To understand how the Corviale void came to be as it is one has to return to Rome's regional plan of 1962. The key issues for the post-war development of the city were infrastructure and affordable housing. These, taken together, were both opportunity and inspiration to radically rethink the form of the city. Unfortunatley, the institutional means for thinking infrastructure and housing together did not exist in Italy in the immediate post-war period. It only became possible to think them together after 1952, when the ministry of public works adopted a regional planning policy. In the particular case of Rome, it then took ten more years of debate and discussion to arrive at an acceptable regional plan for the strategic development of the city.

By 1962 Rome had been the subject of much post-war development, but on the basis of an old, pre-war plan. The pre-war plan encouraged rapid but sporadic forms of development in all areas of the city, but it was not suited for thinking infrastructure and housing together. Along with the initiatives that would eventually lead to the construction of Corviale, the 1962 plan was conducive to the simultaneous thinking of infrastructure and housing, giving rise to new ideas for built form. One such new idea concerned the building of what, in effect, would have been a second city centre, located just to the east of the historic city. Known as the Sistema Direzionale Orientale (Eastern Business and Administrative System), the new city center was conceived as an environmental system, rather than a traditional urban core. As its name suggested, it was to function as a business and administrative quarter, its key structuring idea was the Asse Attrezzato (equipped axis as the term translates into English).[13] But the city failed to act on the idea.

Confronted by the city's incapacity to act, a number of Roman architects formed a collaborative group to work on a speculative proposal for the Asse Attrezzato.[14] Calling themselves The Asse Studio, the collaborators worked together, from 1967 through to 1970. In justifying their decision to work together, unsolicited and for free, the group explained it was the only option open to them. Because, as is often the case for architects, on the one hand they wanted to express their dissatisfaction with the political factors determining the production of the built environment in Rome, yet on the other they did not want to abandon their commitment to design.

One member of the Asse Studio, an architect named Mario Fiorentino, eventually became the lead designer and project manager for Corviale. Fiorentino worked on Corviale from its conception in 1972 right through to 1982, when building work ceased. In moving from the speculative project for the Asse Attrezzato to the real project for designing and building Corviale, Fiorentino took with him a whole new set of ideas about the relationship between architecture and infrastructure. These were ideas that he and his colleagues had invented and explored as they worked on the Asse Attrezzatto.

Although the Asse Studio finished working on the Asse Attrezzato in 1970, it was not until 1975 that their design research was finally published, by which time work on Corviale had been in progress for 3 years. The research was published in a special issue of the journal *L'architettura, Cronache e Storia, (no. 238-239)* (figure 8). The utopian impulse behind the research is made abundantly clear in the journal's editorial statement:

This special issue is devoted to the archaeologists of the year 3100 and later. It will be good for them to know about the causes of the urban disaster of the 1960-'80 period. The Rome city plan, approved in 1962, incorporated a great and resolving idea: an 'Asse Attrezzato' (throughway) which, beginning at the terminal of the superhighway from Florence, linked to the new Pietralata and Centocelle business districts and then, connecting to the EUR district, led into the superhighway of the Sun for Naples. This spinal road, located in the city's eastern sector, would have had three effects: a) saving the historic core, b) setting in motion a process of renovation of the shabby peripheral sectors, and c) imparting on the city an organic and modern image. Although the plan was praised by ministers, mayors, administrators, men of culture and journalists... nothing was done to put it into effect. In an extreme attempt to jolt the authorities out of their inactivity, a team of architects has developed an extensive research, which evidences the feasibility of the 'Asse.' We publish the essential parts of this research; it will show the archaeologists that, in the XX century, not everybody surrendered in the face of Rome's ruin.[15]

By appealing to fictional readers - the archeologists of the future - the editorial statement has the effect of drawing the actual reader of the journal into a curious relationship with the text (curious that is for an architectural journal). The allusion to a future generation of archeologists has something magical about it, taking the reader's imagination into another world, projected from the present into the future. And yet the projected world is disturbing, because in it the reader is asked to imagine a future Rome in ruins.

By using the editrorial statement to frame their research the Asse Studio were emulating the publicity techniques we have already seen in Piranesi's

Figure 8

L'architettura, Cronache e Storia, (no. 238-239), front cover

presentation of his proposal for the Campo Marzio. Just like the Scenographia, the reference to the future makes the research seem magical and at the same time disturbing, in effect it dislocates the reader from their familiar frame of reference, obliging them to think twice about the status of the research.

The Asse Attrezzato

In the visual material representing the design of the Asse Attrezzato we can see an underlying hexagonal geometry, it appears as a continuous grid of isosceles triangles, marked on the ground datum represented in the model and plan-diagrams (figure 9). There are other geometrical figures meshed with the hexagonal grid, these take the form of bars, circles, triangles, octagons and hexagons, they fuse together to form an enormous construction (figure 10). In the section drawings the geometric figures completely disappear. The over-riding quality of the Asse Attrezzato seen in section is that of an all pervasive striped-ness. It appears as a laminated mass in which horizontal vectors represent constructed floor-plates, stacked one above the other at equal intervals, the entire aggregate floating over the indented datum of the ground plane (figure 11).

In the light of Fiorentino's subsequent involvement in the Corviale development, the Asse Studio's repertoire of shapes, relationships and their figural aggregations is especially interesting, because they hint at the ancestry of the shapes, relationships and figural aggregations that came to characterise Corviale; and can be seen today from a satellite view in Google Earth, or from an aeroplane flying into the city (figure 12).

In gazing upon Corviale from the air, what is striking is the way it appears to combine extraordinary size and extreme simplicity. In the aerial image of Rome, Corviale operates at the same scale as the iconic monuments, such as St Peter's, the Piazza Navona, the Colosseum. But Corviale is notably different to these world famous forms. The compositional principles it has inherited from its Asse Attrezzato ancestor are clearly visible in the aerial image and cause Corviale to stand out as belonging to an altogether different way of thinking about architecture and environment. To find out more about that difference it is necessary to return to the Asse Studio's research and take a closer look.

In the drawings and models, the Asse Attrezzato appears as a network of vectors, rather than a compact form. It has a dominant north-south direction, punctuated by four nodes, each one with its own distinct planimetric configuration. One node is square, one is triangular, one is diamond-shaped and one is circular. From each node a network of vectors splits away from the main north-south trajectory and diffuses, in diverse directions, into the surrounding landscape. What is striking about this configuration is the way it seems

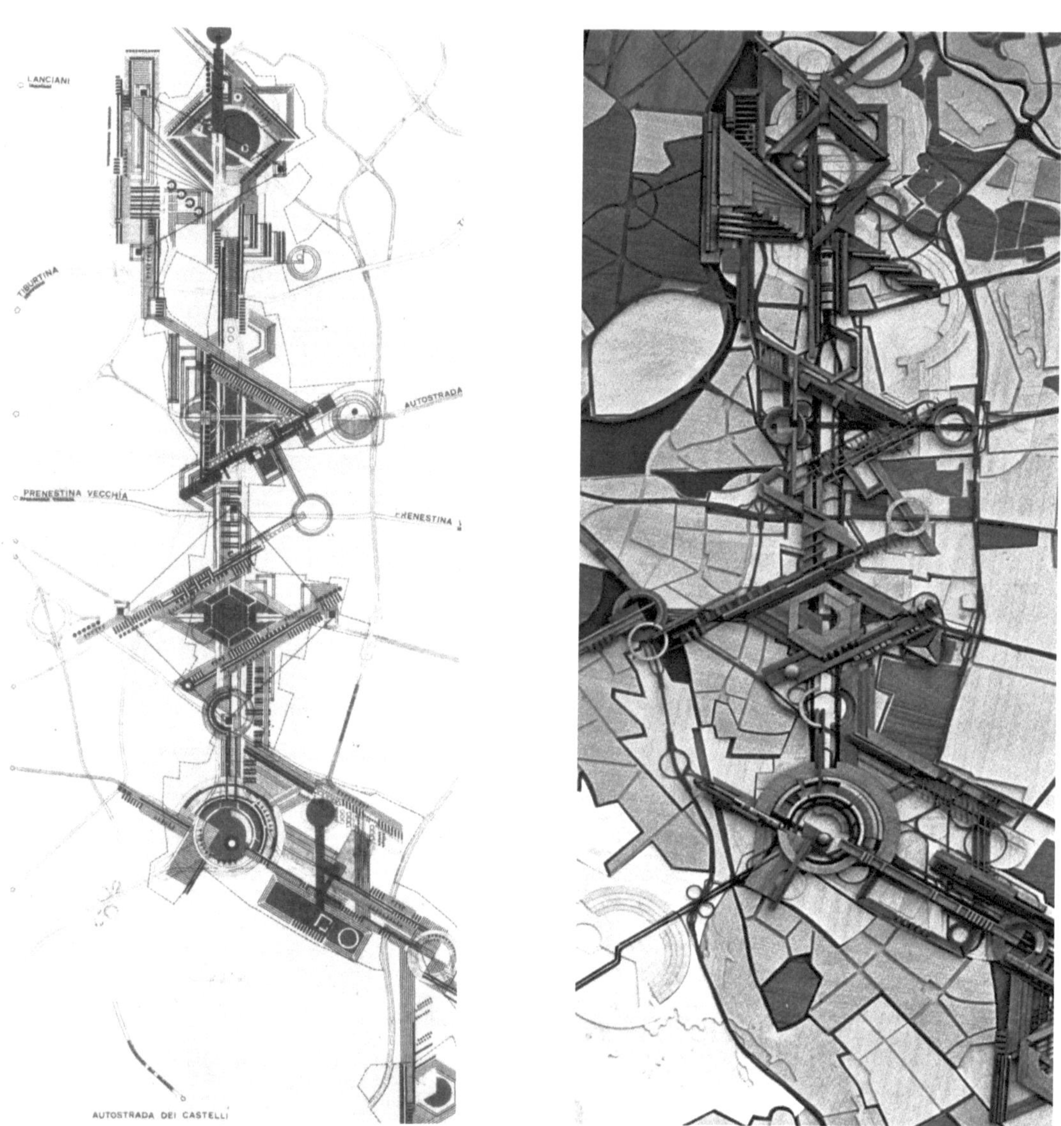

Figure 9

The architects conceived the Asse Attrezzato as a single system of roads and buildings aggregated into one monstrous artefact

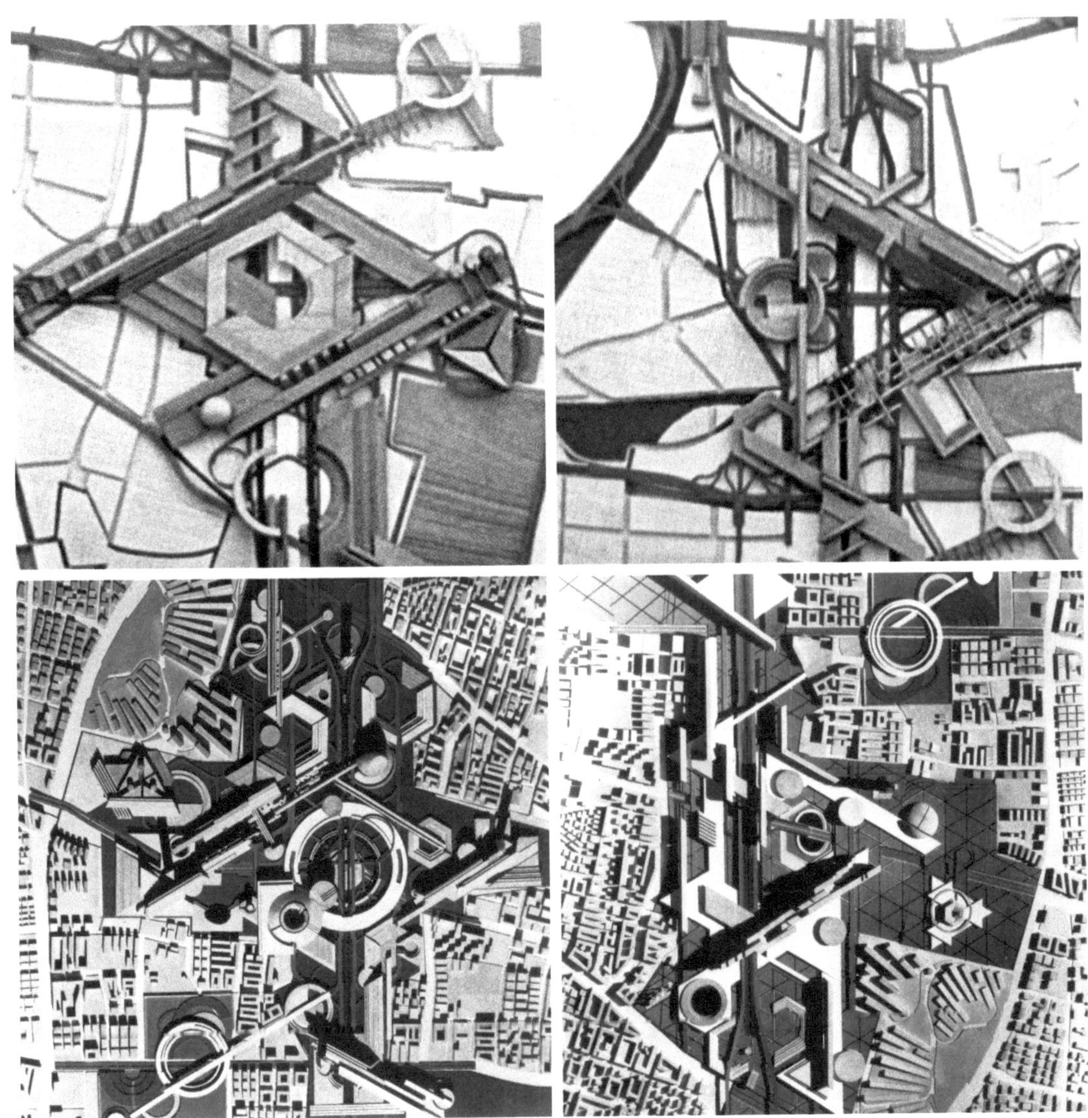

Figure 10

Plan projections showing the geometrical figures that fuse together to form the Asse Attrezzato - bars, circles, octagons and hexagons

Figure 11

In sectional projections the Asse Attrezzato appears as a laminated mass with horizontal vectors representing constructed floor plates, stacked one above the other, at equal intervals. The entire aggregate floats over the undulating surface of the ground plane

Figure 12

Corviale, located on an aerial view (above) and as seen in a satellite view in Google Earth (below)

to merge roads and buildings into a single, enormous artefact. It is as if the architects had envisaged new kinds of relationships between the inside and the outside of buildings, including the circulation of human bodies, and vehicles, around and through them. As the architects themselves described it, what they were proposing was not so much a composition *'of isolated, single purpose buildings,'* but an amalgam of *'fluid building volumes, interconnected and complex,'* a sort of promenade for bodies and vehicles on a very large scale, one that would be *'rich in green space and dense with communication on all levels.'*[16]

The architects' description of their fluid building volumes identifies four different kinds of spatial relationship, each of which is expressed as a discrete type. The set of relationships is structured around the opposition indoors/outdoors. At one extreme is the type *'all-outdoors,'* at the other extreme, its opposite, *'all-indoors.'* In between these limits there are two hybrid types, one that is *'outdoors but shaded'* and another that is *'outdoors-indoors.'*[17] The last of these is immediately recognisable as the prototypical idea of the Corviale void.

Since its completion in 1982, Corviale has been criticised for its inadequate functioning as a place to live. In the early 2,000s, several proposals were drawn-up for its improvement. One common feature of all the proposals was the way they ignored the architectural history of the void, most notably they neglected the origins of the void in the work of the Asse Studio.

For example, in 2007 there were a number of suggestions for reconfiguring the block, proposing the apartments be converted into units fitting snuggly within the building's cross-wall system.[18] At Corviale's conception and as the appartments were built, they were arranged either side of the void. This meant that all views out were mono-directional. For apartments on the eastern side all views looked out towards the city, on the western side towards the country. In the proposals for reconfiguring the block the apartments were to be turned through 90 degrees and made to run in the other direction, spanning across the void from east to west, each one enjoying double aspect views (figure 13, top image).

Alongside the proposals for reconfiguration and in the name of a movement calling itself *New Urbanism*, a number of proposals were made to demolish the block completely and replace it with 3-5 storey buildings. The new buildings were to be arranged as loosely grouped blocks around an open central garden space. The New Urbanists justified their hostility toward the void by the simple fact that they did not like the approach to urbanism and architecture it represented. Instead they prefered the pre-war approach, which they mistook

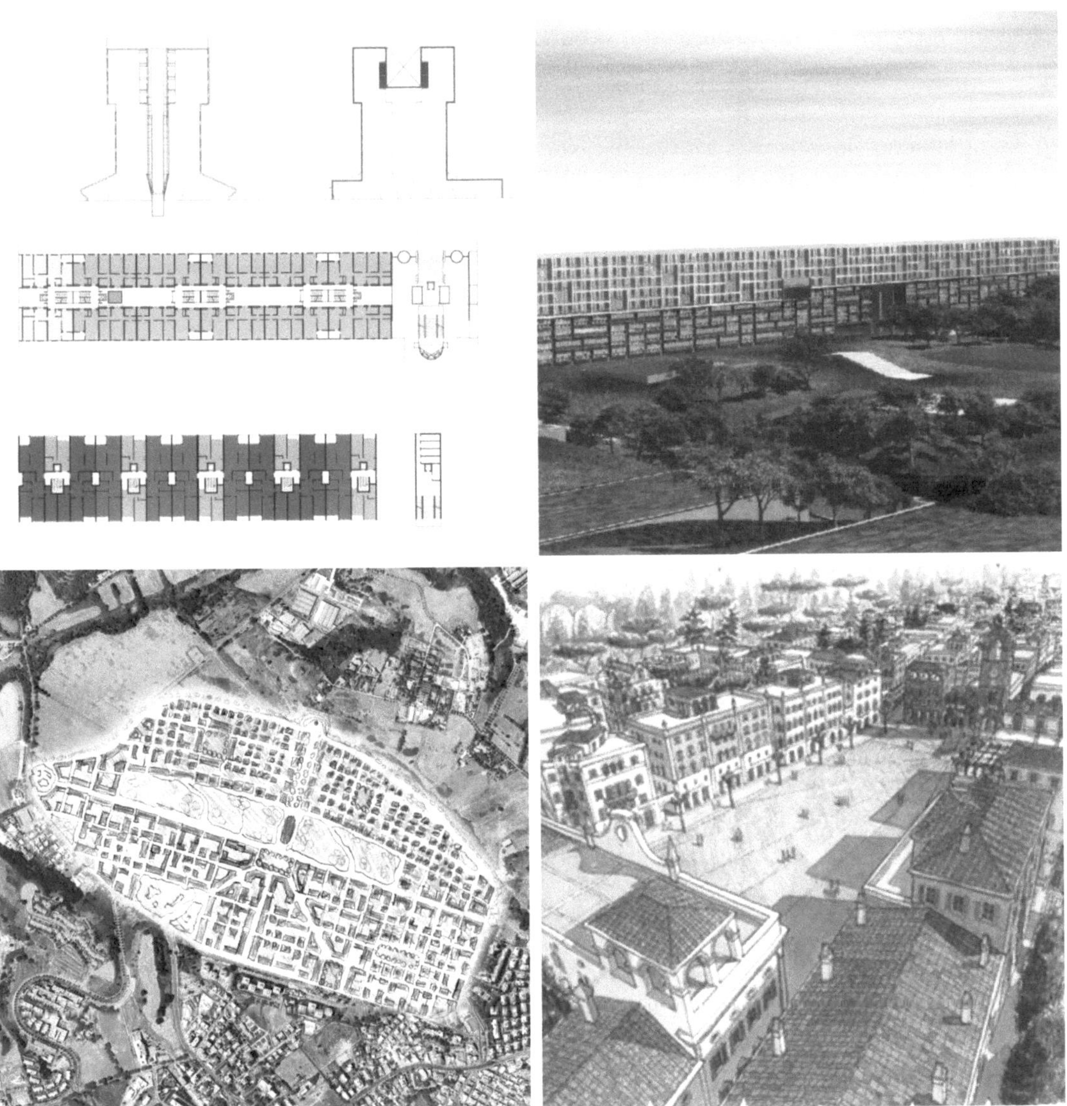

Figure 13

Proposals for the regeneration of Corviale, involving reconfiguration of the void (above) and total demolition (below)

for a long standing tradition in architectural and urban thinking (figure 13, bottom image).[19]

Both strategies for altering Corviale were formally quite different, yet each one deployed architectural design as a means of eliminating the critique of infrastructure and building that was the basis of the Corviale strategy. As a consequence, neither approach was the least bit interested in preserving Corviale's most notable feature, namely the void. They were blind to the legitimate claim that Corviale is a unique expression of twentieth century thinking about architecture and environment and as such, has heritage value and deserves consideration as a potential candidate for preservation.

Proposal

In what follows we (Doctor Watson Architects) will describe our proposal for preserving the Corviale void. We formulated the proposal in 2010, our aim was to publicise the void (in the Utopian sense introduced above), thus making it appear more vivedly than it did at the time. We believed a vivified void would contribute more positively to the architecture of Rome and the metropolitan region than an eradicated void.

Taking Piranesi's Campo Marzio as a working model, our proposal began with the establishment of a Topografia, the operative metaphor for what we were doing at this stage was 'taking-away.' The first thing to be removed was Corviale's housing function. It was not our intention to make the residents homeless and so we proposed to re-house them in one of the new, paradigmatic megastructure units that had recently been proposed as part of a strategic urban design study, formulated as a critique of the 2008 master plan for Rome. The proposal in question was entitled *The Centre(s) Elsewhere*, henceforth referred to as CCE.[20]

As well as offering a strategy for improving the system of public transport within the city territory, the CCE proposed a number of new, garden/megastructure units, each one corresponding to one of the six consular roads leading out of the city. A key feature of our proposed Topografia involved interfacing with the CCE's strategic design study to suggest that the Corviale residents be re-housed in the second of the six CCE garden/megastructure units, designed for the consular road nearest to Corviale, i.e. the via Ostiense. The proposed megastructure was to be located very close to the Corviale development, at the spot where the river Tiber comes closest to the Via Ostiense and to the resuscitated rail and tram network, a carefully considered component of the CCE's strategic design (figure 14).[21]

With the housing function removed there was no reason to keep the circulation devices that punctuated the Corviale block and occluded the basic structural pattern.

Figure 14

The second of the CCE's five garden/megastructure units, located on the consular road closest to Corviale, at the spot where the Tiber and via Ostiense almost meet, and to the resuscitated rail and tram network

As already mentioned, the six metre rhythm of cross-wall units is interrupted by five vertical, tower-like structures with horizontal, bridge-like additions. For our purposes the towers and bridges were getting in the way, making it hard to perceive the single-mindedness of the underlying cross-wall system. For Corviale's housing function the towers and bridges were essential, a means of getting from the perimeter of the building to the dwelling units, but with the housing function gone those circulation devices would no longer be necessary.

The removal of the housing function paved the way to a third and fourth act of taking away. The items concerned were the external and internal space-dividing elements that defined and differentiated the apartments. The third removal item was the system of cladding panels, including fixed and opening lights that were applied to the external face of the building and to the balcony fronts facing into the void. The fourth removal item was the system of partitions that divided the apartments into aggregates of rooms, as well as all the doorways and internal fixtures and fittings.

On the basis of the four types of taking-away so far described all that would have remained of the Corviale block was a concrete assembly of vertical cross-walls and horizontal floor-plates. With the building in that condition the void would have appeared as a negative volume, hollowed out from the matrix of cross-walls and floor-plates. The final act of taking away, which would have completed the Topographia, was the removal of the large walls that prohibited ground level access to the void. The net consequence of the five acts of taking-away would have been to expose the void in the manner shown in the drawing on the facing page (figure 15).

By exposing the void as described we thought it would be possible to link it more explicitly to its forgotten history. We were especially keen to draw upon Corviale's utopian heritage in the Asse Studio's proposal for the Asse Attrezzato. Recollect how those architects had begun to imagine new kinds of relationships between interior and exterior space. We were especially interested in their idea of an *'outdoors that is indoors,'*[22] i.e., a space that concretises the idea of outside-in, because we could see that it was the prototypical ancestor of the void. We wanted to celebrate the idea of outside-in and in so doing to give phenomenal and symbolic expression to the void's utopian dimension. To this end we proposed to re-imagine Corviale as a facility for studying the ontology of outside-in-ness (from here on referred to as the FSoOO).

To make the FSoOO properly resistant to the socio-economic forces acting within the contemporary city we believed it necessary to work with all three of Tafuri's strategies for survival in times of crisis. This meant, first

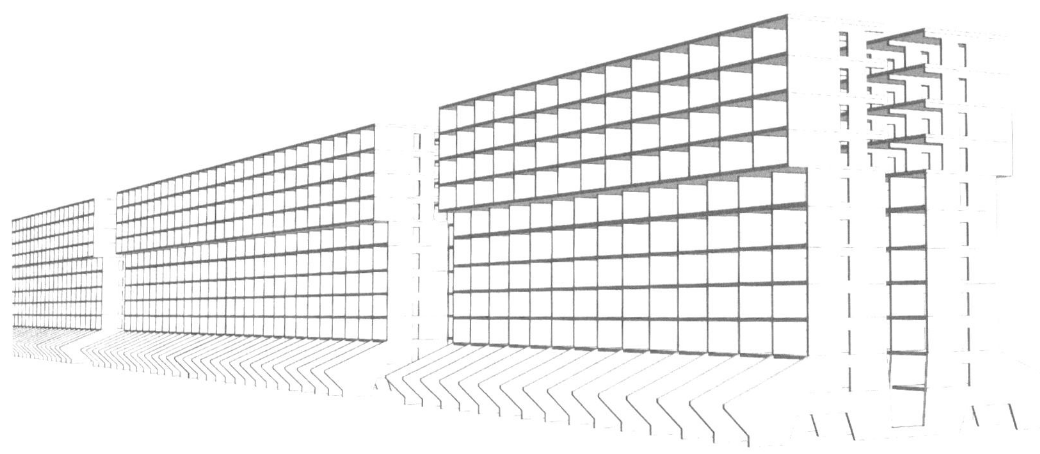

Figure 15

The Corviale block is stripped down to a bare carcass consisting in a concrete matrix of vertical cross-walls and horizontal floor-plates. The void now appears as a missing part, belonging to the order of the matrix but as a negative figure, hollowed out from its overall form.

working with debased materials, second, working in a muted language of expression, i.e., in silence and, third, attracting public attention. The first and second of these were already fulfilled in the proposed acts of taking-away, as set out above, which would have disarticulated the housing function and de-cloaked the void; but the third strategy required something more.

Public Transport

In 2010 the most direct public transport link between the centre of Rome and Corviale was by bus, from Piazza Pasquale. The journey took somewhere in the order of 30 minutes. Already there was something quite grand about it, partly because the bus route terminated at Corviale, but also because of the way the bus was turned round at the end of the journey. Upon reaching its destination the bus made a two kilometre circuit in front of the Corviale building, on a roadway laid out in the familiar shape of an ancient Roman circus (figure 16).

For the FSoOO we decided to treat this existing transport link as a readymade, but to adapt it to enhance the FSoOO's public profile. To this end we proposed, first the route would now pass down the centre of the void, rather than in front of the block, and, second, to replace the existing buses with an electric railway, or tramline. The new line would run through the void at ground level, thereby making it possible to shuttle students, visitors and faculty of the FSoOO from the centre of Rome, out to the void and from one end of the void to the other. The new line would exit at the far, southern-most end of the building, where it would loop round on a continuous circuit laid out in the form of a circus (plate 1). Then it would return, doubling back to travel once again through the void and then head on back to the centre of Rome (plate 2).

In place of the circulation towers, removed in the preparatory Topographic works, we proposed to install five - one for each location - small stations as stopping off points along the new line (plate 3). Each station was to have two small platforms, one either side of the track, a number of ticket machines, an automated cashpoint and a small pavilion, or kiosk, for the purchase of light refreshments and provision for internet connectivity (plate 4). Each station would be equipped with two elevators, one either side of the line (plate 5). The elevator cars would be transparent, open and light (as would the tramcars) and large enough for at least 15 people to use at any one time (plate 6). The elevators would provide a means of vertical circulation, up and into the concrete matrix of the block, right up to the rooftop (plate 7).

The introduction of public transport into the void would have satisfied our objective of introducing an outside into the void (plate 8), but that was not our main reason

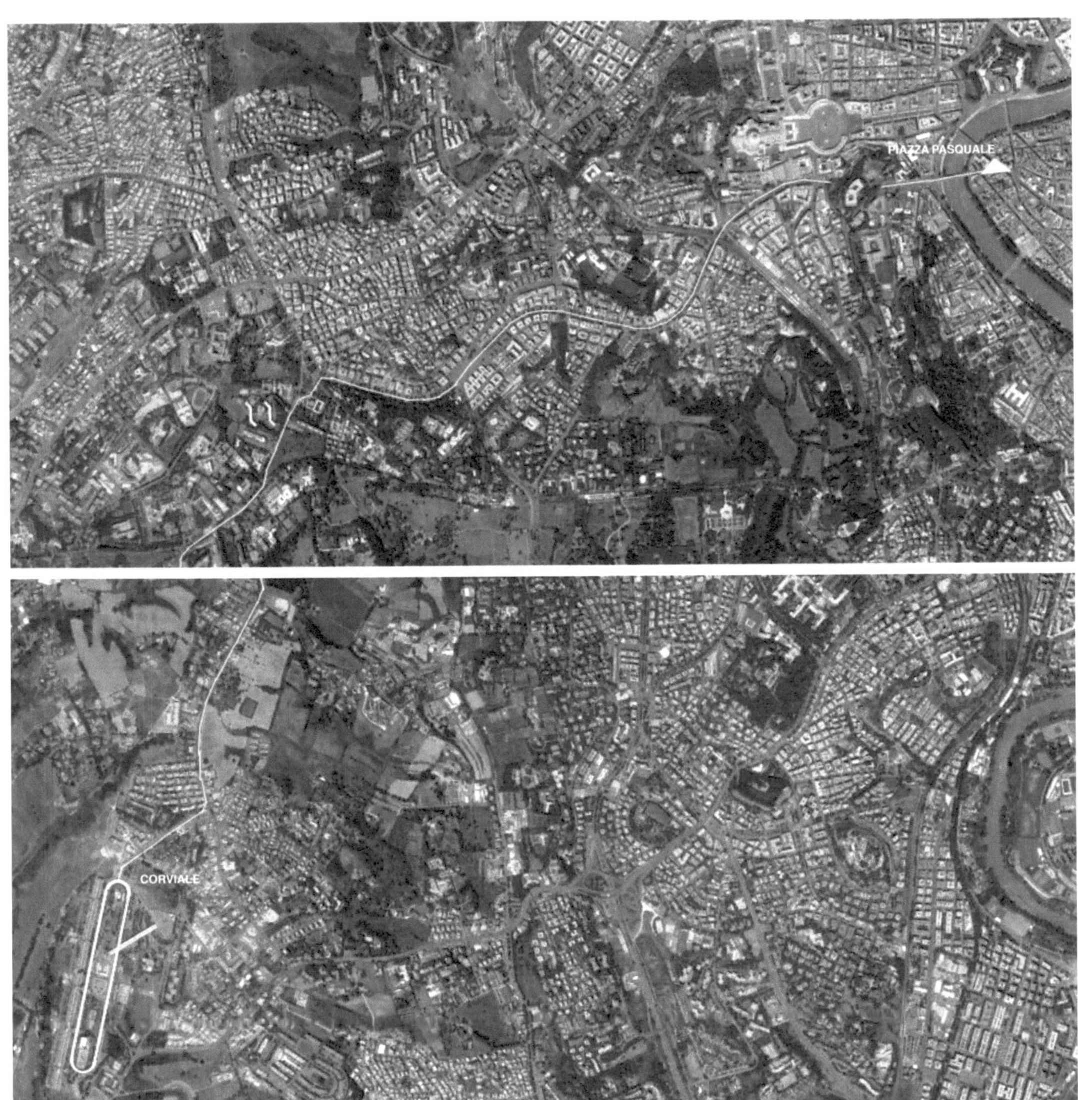

Figure 16

The most convenient public transport link between the centre of Rome and Corviale was by but, from Piaza Pasquale, the journey took about 30 minutes

for installing it. The reason we wanted to bring public transport right into the very heart of the building was because we intended to put something in there that was desirable for people to see (plate 9). To explain our ideas for what that desirable something was it is necessary to return once again to Piranesi's Ichnographiam Campi Martii Antique Urbis.

The marvellous six plate ensemble is the centre piece of Piranesi's Campo Marzio, without it the other drawings, beautiful though they are, would be ineffective. It is hard to be certain why the Ichnographiam attracts attention in quite the way it does, its form and texture seem to act as a kind of magnet for human eyes. Irrespective of its utopian content, the Ichnographiam is materially attractive, it is evocative of Plato's *real world,* where colours and forms are no longer ideal but tactile and dazzling.[23] Piranesi's bold manner of working on his etchings produced a voluminous, optically tactile imagery that is attractive to the eye - surely one reason for the lure of the Ichnographiam. Another reason is the extraordinary variety among the plan figures of the buildings spread across the Campo. As a total ensemble they constitute a tumultuous aggregation of lines, shapes and relationships.

Whatever the causes of the Ichnographiam's power, we felt that the Corviale void should be endowed with an equivalent detailed and dazzling materiality. The clue as to how to devise an economy of dazzling materiality for the void came to us via the Asse Studio's notion of the fluid volume.[24] The Corviale void is a negative space, full of air, and thus already a fluid volume, but air inside buildings is transparent and does not carry the same connotations as air outside. The symbolic form for outside air is the sky, which is perceived as a vast expanse of film blue, an expanse that recedes upwards, away from the gaze of the viewer; at least that is so in the daytime. At night the sky disappears and so too, in a certain sense, does the air, although people continue to breath!

We wanted to express the air inside the void as palpable. To this end we decided to render the void in the same concrete manner Piranesi had rendered the Campo Marzio. Except, instead of working with the medium of etched and printed line and building plans as Piranesi had done, we invented a new medium to work with.

Beetles

In order to render the void palpable we devised a new colour form. It was based on the idea of a swarm or a shoal, rather than a classical organic body. The new form was to be made out of millions of individual units, here on referred to as 'beetles.' We conceived the beetle as a tiny robot-computer that could fly. We imagined the body of the beetle would be a simple wire frame, made of three elemental body parts. Each part would express one of the spatial triad X, Y & Z, and would structure a small portion of three-dimensional space (plate 10).

The beetles were to be tiny, their body parts measuring no more than 9 millimetres in length. In a sense they would be to the void what the hatched lines are to Piranesi's Ichnographiam. However, unlike the etched lines of the Ichnographiam, the beetles would be able to move around and to exchange messages amongst themselves, all-be-it of a very simple, rudimentary kind.

Each beetle was to be programmed to respond to a specific feature of its environment, that being the radiating messages from the bodies of other beetles nearby. The activity of any one beetle would have been the expression of its relationship to all the other members of the total beetle population, including their relationships to one another. This meant, first, the beetle population, although constituted out of millions of individuals, would have had a single identity; second, the identity of any one single beetle would have been subsumed within the identity of the total population.

Although the beetle would be programmed to act as an individual with low-level stimulus orientated act/react behaviour, because the beetles, taken en-masse, would have been mutually stimulating, so together they would have formed a population network with emergent behaviour. Although no single beetle would have had any idea of what the group was trying to accomplish (indeed, the notion of accomplishment would have been entirely alien to the beetle population) the population would work together to form simple structures that the students, visitors and faculty of the FSoOO would experience as a continuously changing colour form (plate 11).

The basic principles that would have been used to programme beetle behaviour involved mapping the X, Y & Z co-ordinates of the beetle body onto the directed channels of terrestrial movement: up/down; east/west; north/south. Then, each channel was to be mapped onto the opponent pair colour system that structures human vision: black/white; blue/yellow; red/green.[25] The X, Y & Z beetle body parts would in themselves have been colourless, but they would become coloured as an expression of the beetle's movement through space: up/down=black/white; east/west=blue/yellow and north/south=red/green. For the individual beetle this would have meant that although it felt all the other colours as potentialities, its outward colour appearance would be specified as follows:

a beetle flying upwards would look totally black (plate 12)

a beetle flying downwards would look totally white (plate 13) a beetle flying eastwards would look totally blue (plate 14)

a beetle flying westwards would look totally yellow (plate 15)

a beetle flying northwards would look totally red (plate 16)

a beetle flying southwards would look totally green (plate 17).

The simple rule governing the need to communicate amongst the beetles was to have been the avoidance of direct colour contrast, or, to put it another way, the avoidance of colour antagonism. This meant a beetle travelling in a specific direction, in some specific colour channel, would not have been able to occupy the same body-space as a beetle travelling in the same colour channel but moving in the opposite direction. For example, a beetle flying blackly upwards would have to switch colour channel in order to avoid a beetle flying whitely downwards. Or, to take another example, a beetle flying bluely eastwards would have to switch colour channel in order to avoid a beetle flying yellowly westwards.

The assessment of colour antagonism risk (CAR) would have depended on the beetles capacity to read proximal body space, a region of sensitivity measured in beetle body lengths. As a consequence, any beetle falling outside the measure of some other beetle's body space could only have been known to it indirectly. The medium of communication being the influence of the other beetle on third party beetles falling in-between. Beetles would be directly aware of other members of the population within a radius of two beetle bodies, which meant the turning-circle of their colour-swerves (the movements beetles would make in order to change colour channel and so avoid colour antagonism) would have been tiny. Thanks to the tiny radius, changes of direction amidst the beetle population would have appeared to human eyes as flecks of changing colour. To human eyes the beetle population would have sparked with flecks of colour as beetles swerved to switch channels and avoid antagonising one another through colour contrast.

A beetle would have been programmed with switching preferences and would always change into a different colour-channel before it would reverse colour-direction. In the scenario in which a black/up beetle was heading for colour contrast with a white/down, the decision as to which one should switch would have been made by weighing up the options jointly available to them and deciding between them what was for the best. If, for example, the blackly upward was blocked from switching, because to do so would have provoked colour antagonism in other channels, then the whitely downward would have switched channel in order to avoid the impending antagonism in white and black. Where beetles from different colour channels crossed paths there would have been no danger of colour contrast and they would have momentarily merged to create a colour event.

As we have already mentioned, students, visitors and faculty of the FSoOO would have experienced the beetles en masse as a unified form, woven into a diaphanous whole, rather in the way a cloud, a flock of birds, or swarm of locusts are perceived as shifting bodies in space.

But students, visitors and faculty could also direct their attention toward localised parts of the beetle mass. With directed attention the viewer would see particular colour events. These would sometimes appear inhibiting, resulting in that region of the mass looking dreary, less dazzling than all the rest. However, there would also be occasions where colour events within a locality were mutually reinforcing. That locality would then appear dazzling (plates 18, 19 & 20). On occasions where the proportion of dazzling to dreary localities was low, the void would have seemed depressed, rather like the sky on a grey, overcast day. On the other hand, with the predominance of dazzle, the appearance of the void would have induced feelings of intense aesthetic pleasure, or bliss.

PLATE 1

The tramline runs through the void at ground level, making it possible to shuttle students, visitors and faculty of the FSoOO from the centre of Rome, out to Corviale and then from one end of the void to the other.

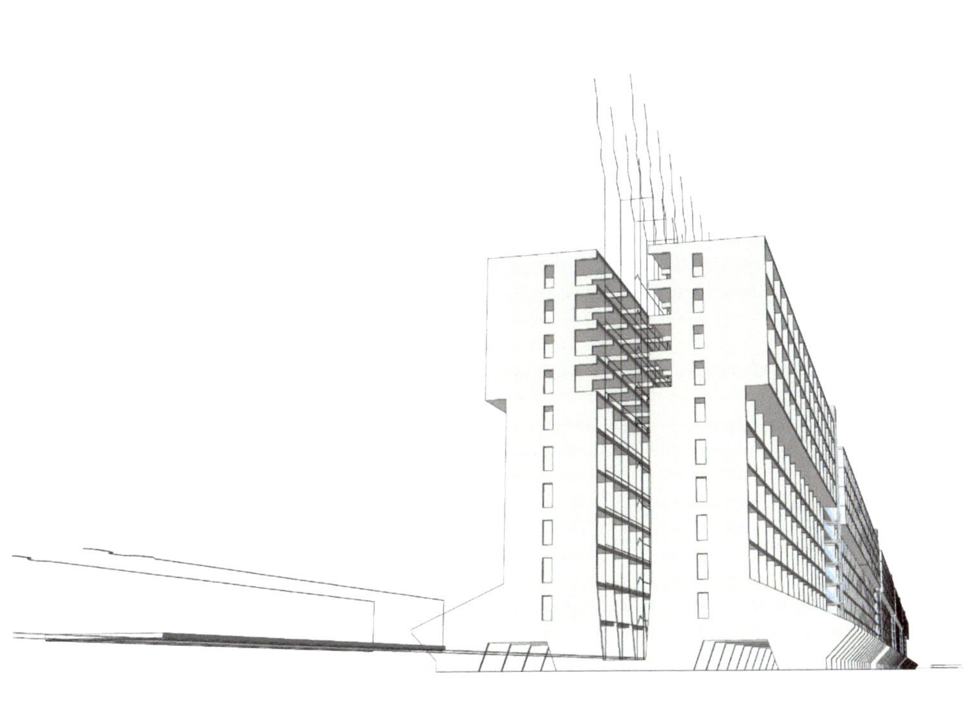

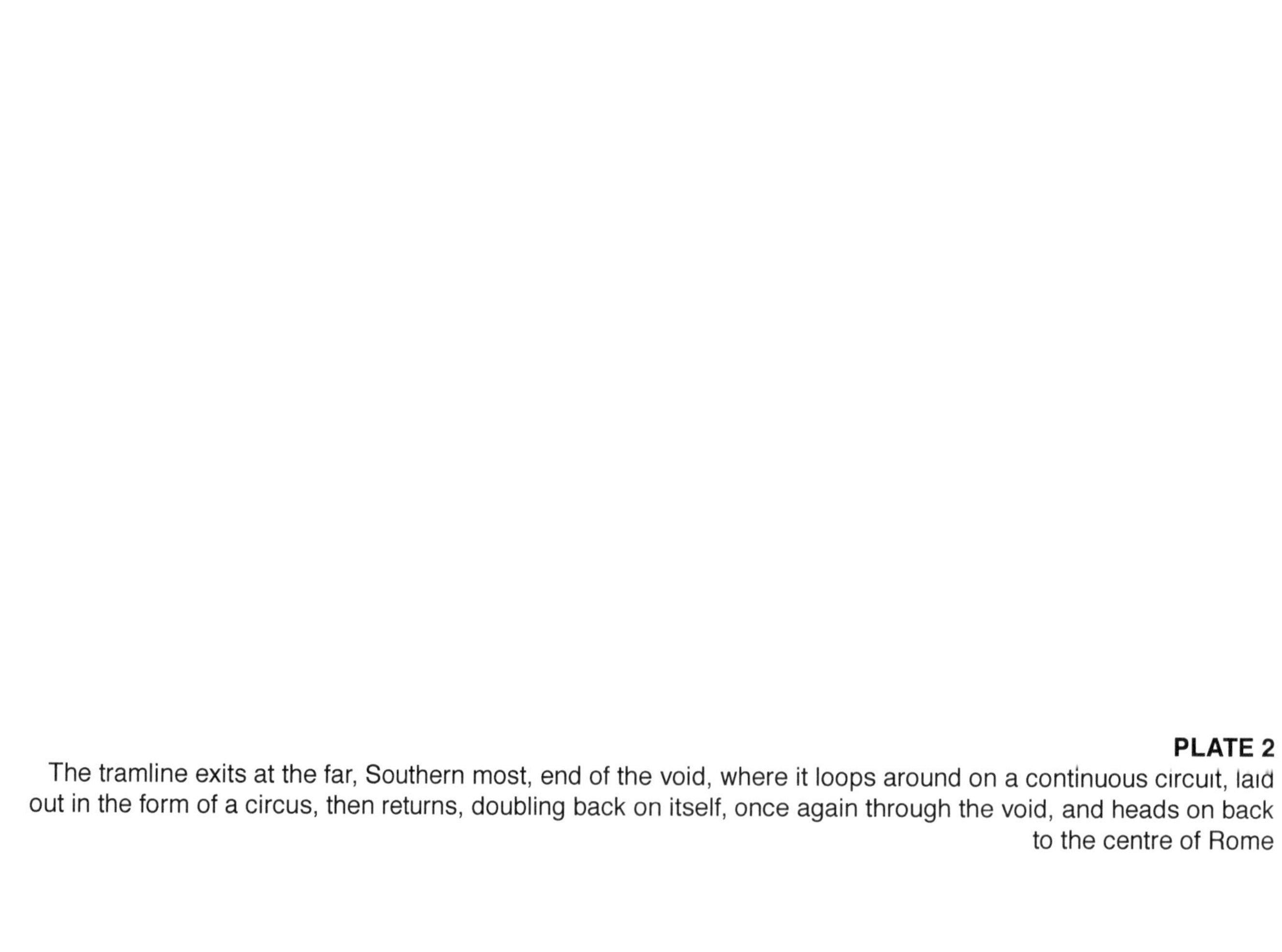

PLATE 2

The tramline exits at the far, Southern most, end of the void, where it loops around on a continuous circuit, laid out in the form of a circus, then returns, doubling back on itself, once again through the void, and heads on back to the centre of Rome

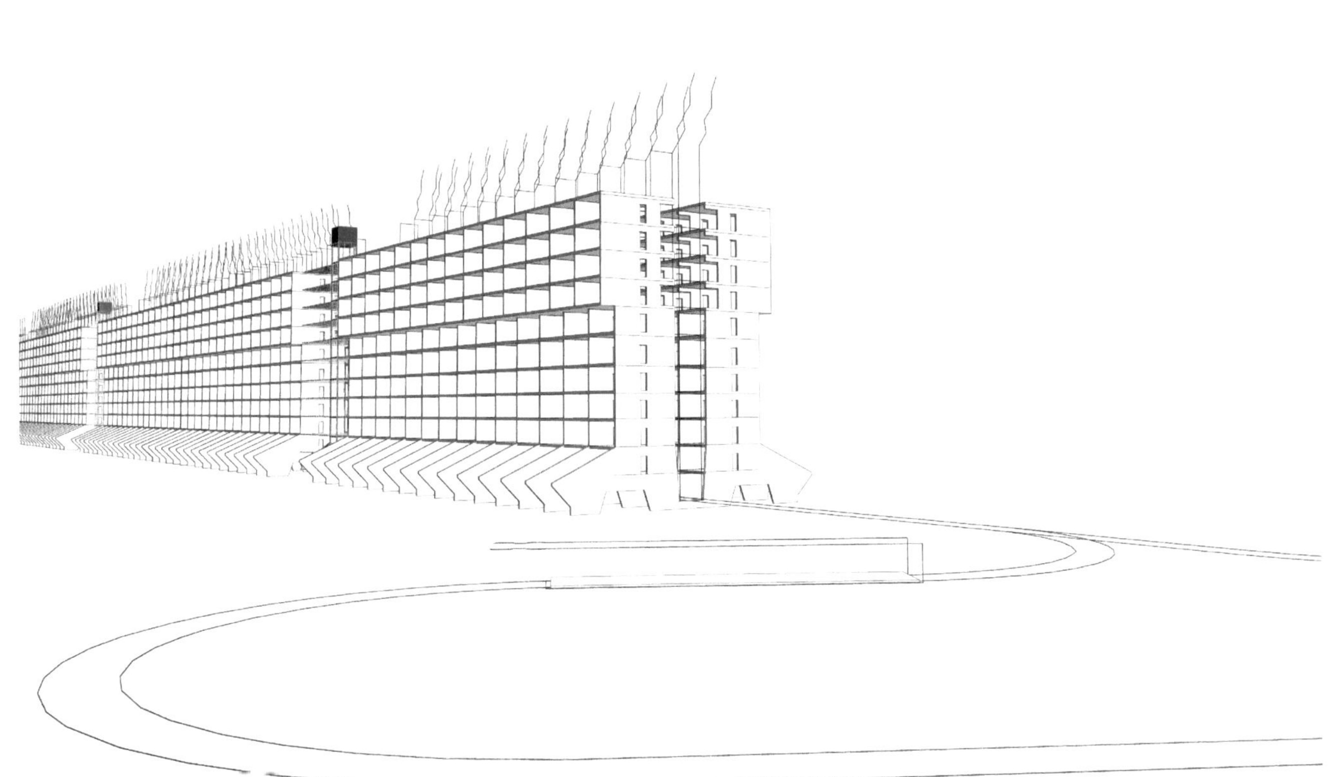

PLATE 3

The rhythm of the towers belongs to the order of the concrete matrix, it is conceptualised as a subtraction from that form. In the place of the removed towers, it is proposed to install five - one for each location - small stations as stopping off points along the tramline

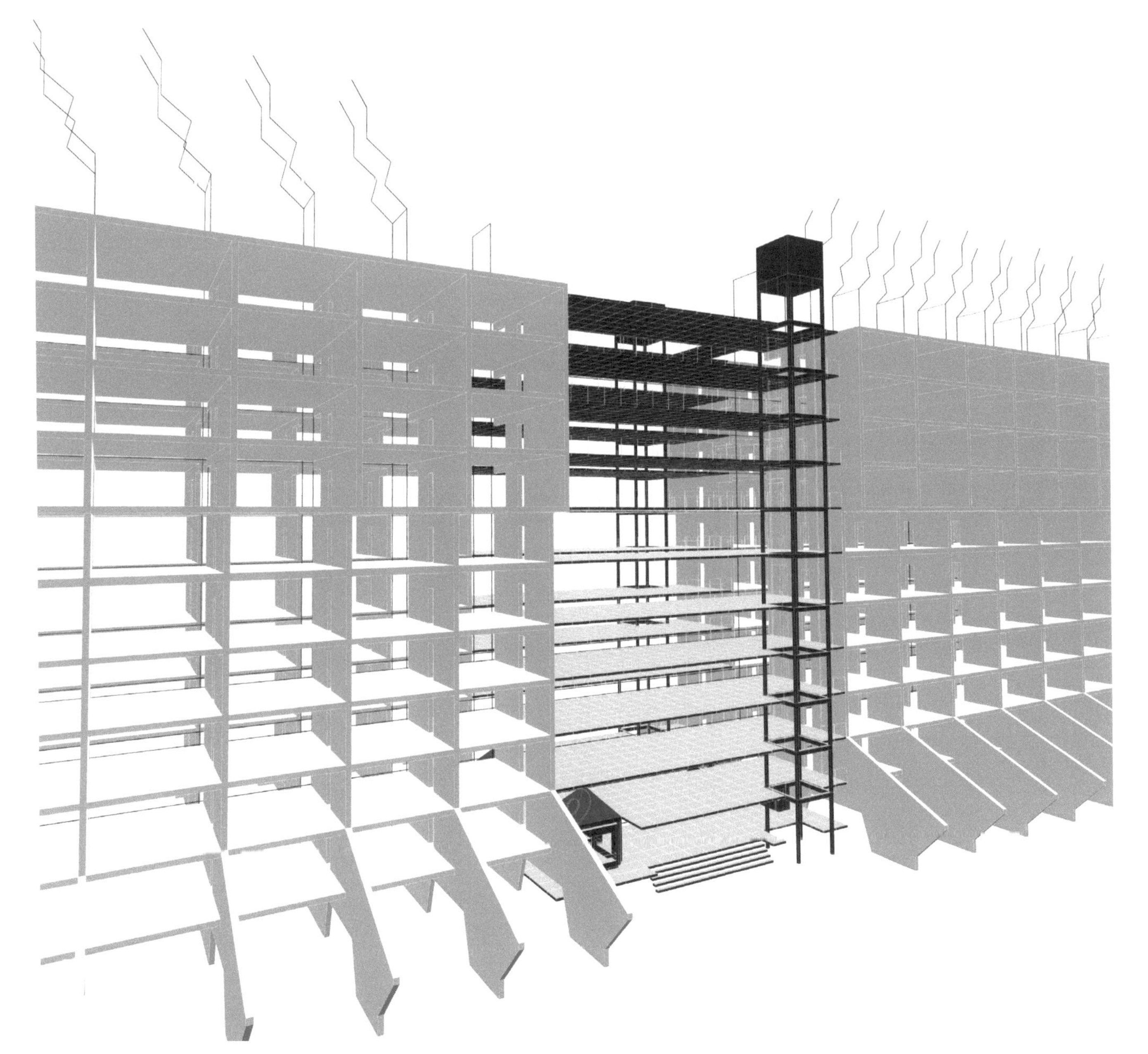

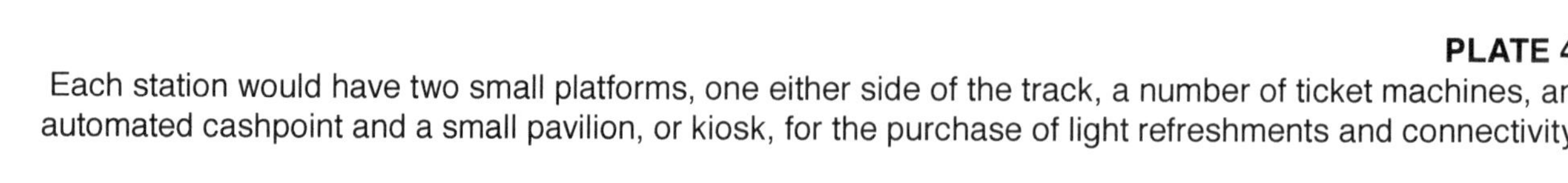

PLATE 4

Each station would have two small platforms, one either side of the track, a number of ticket machines, an automated cashpoint and a small pavilion, or kiosk, for the purchase of light refreshments and connectivity

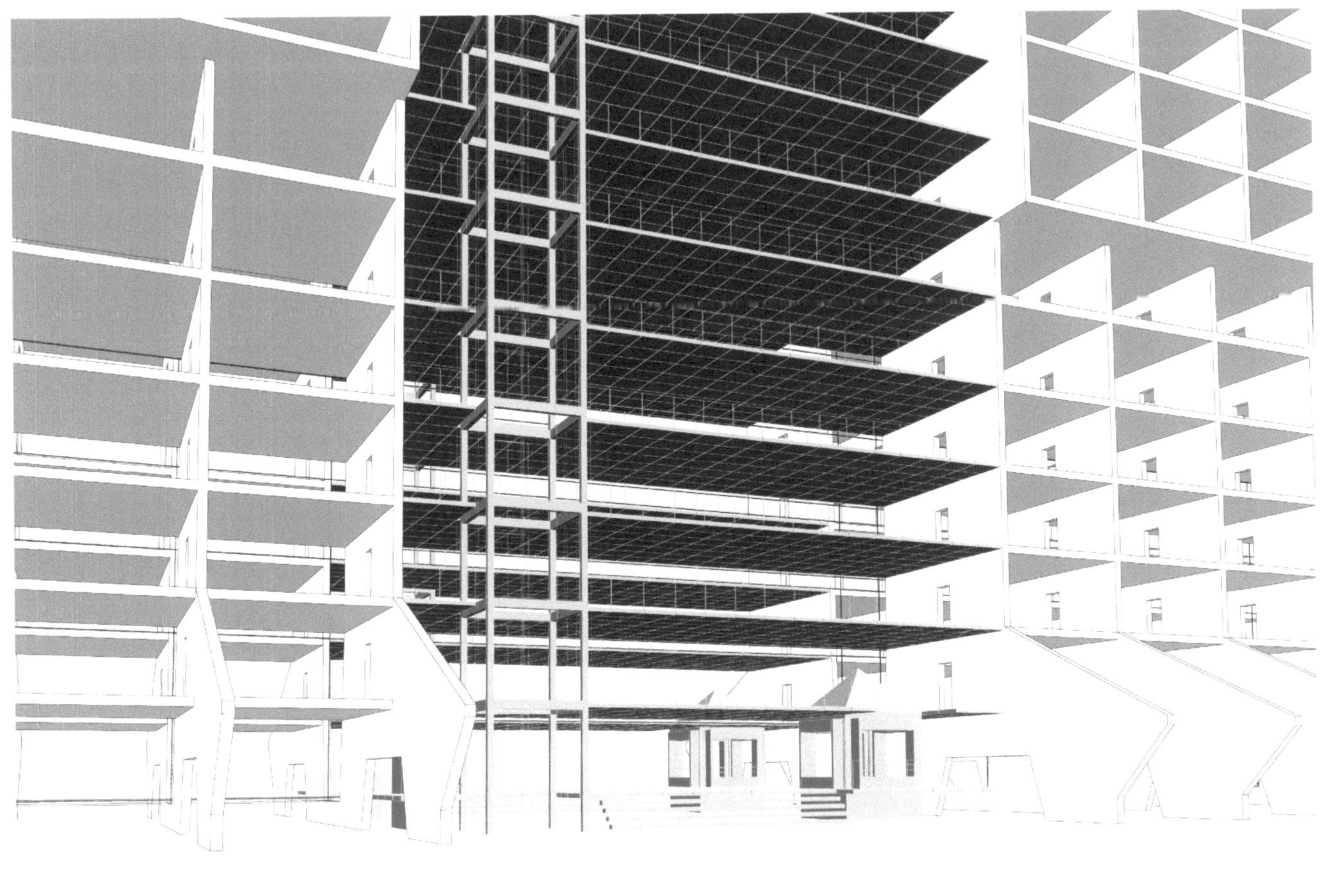

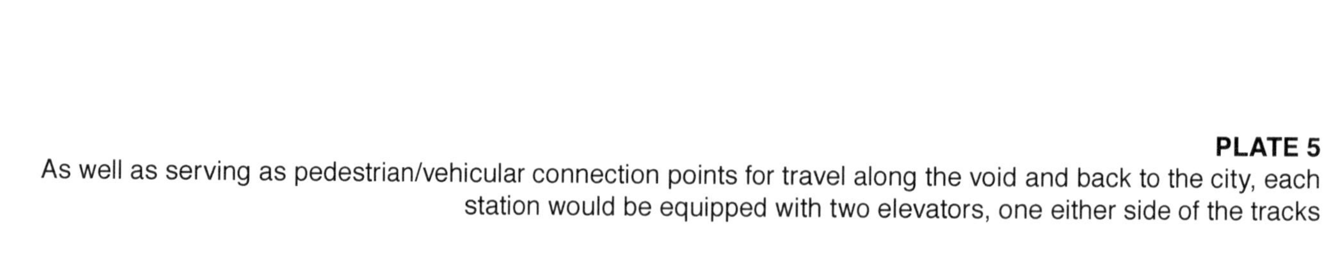

PLATE 5
As well as serving as pedestrian/vehicular connection points for travel along the void and back to the city, each station would be equipped with two elevators, one either side of the tracks

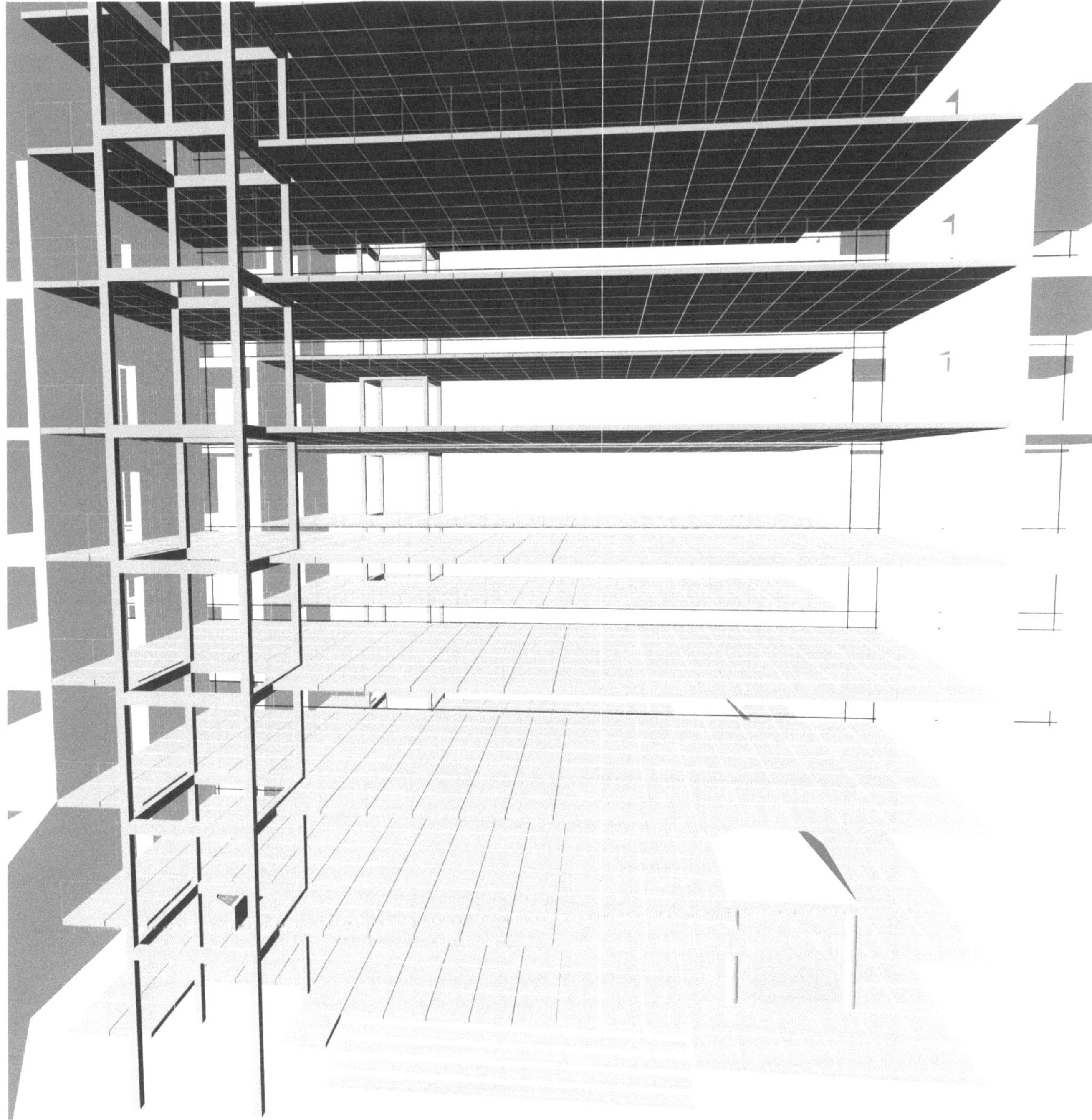

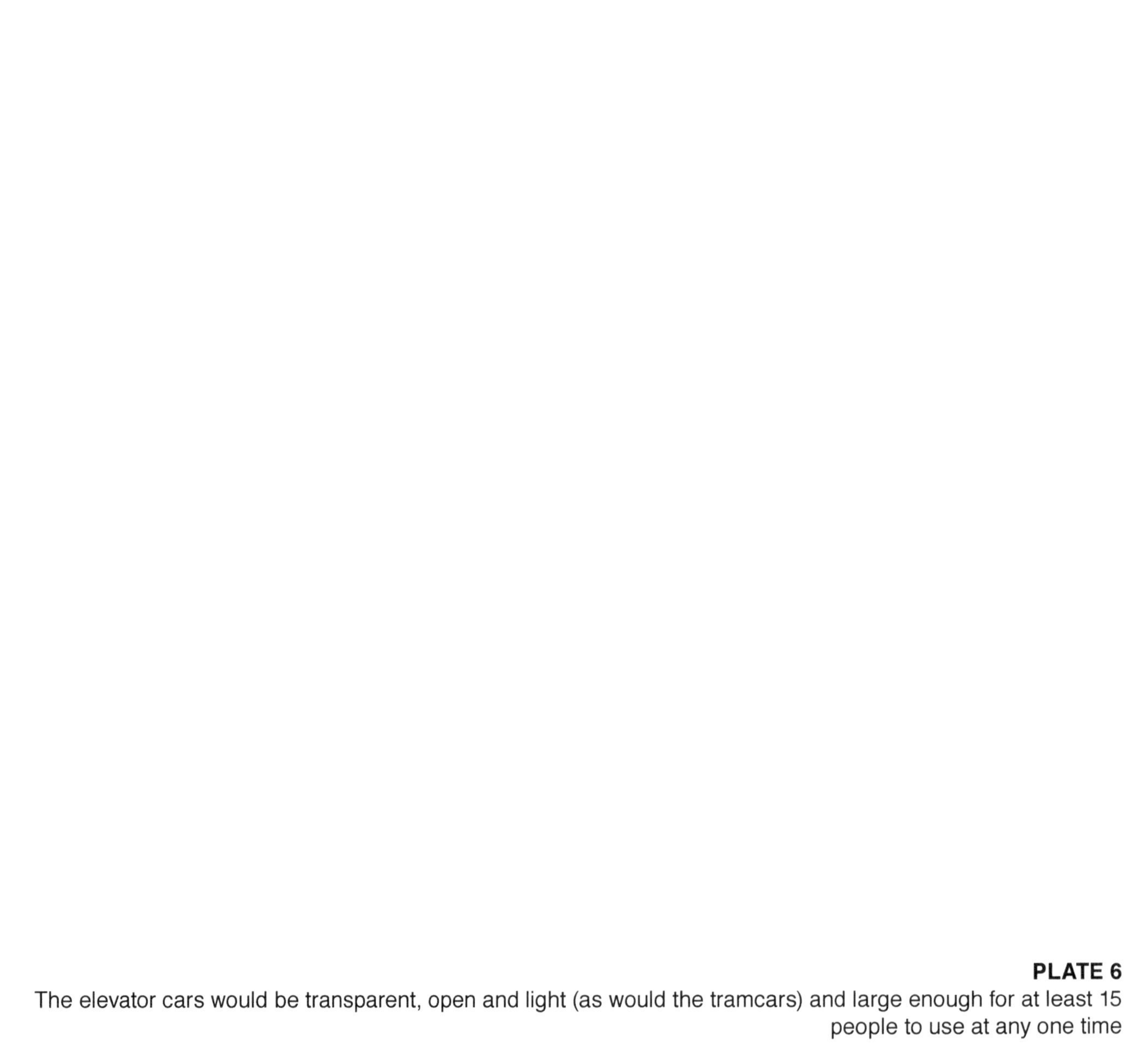

PLATE 6
The elevator cars would be transparent, open and light (as would the tramcars) and large enough for at least 15 people to use at any one time

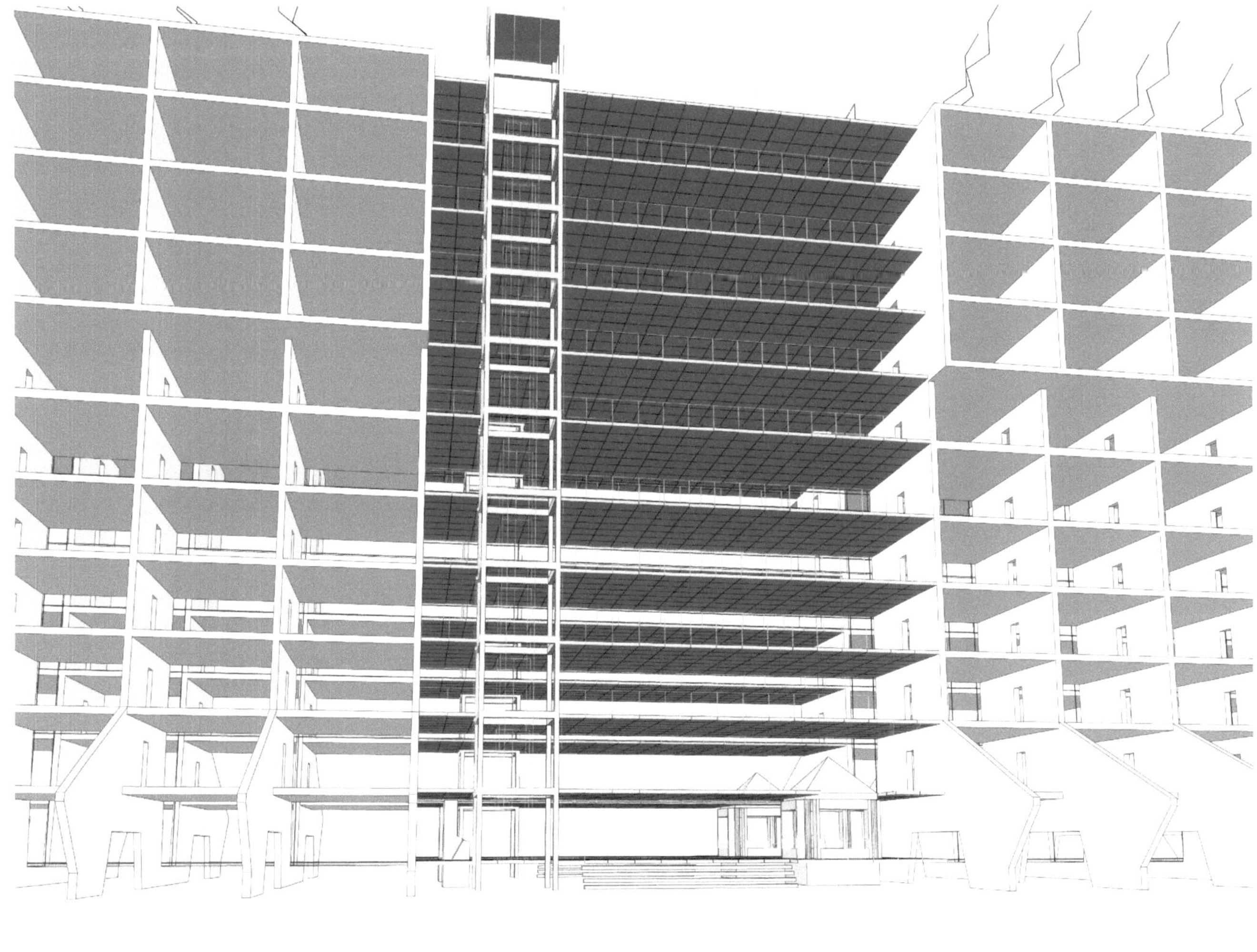

PLATE 7
The purpose of the elevators is to provide a means of public circulation, vertically, up and into the concrete matrix of the building, including the rooftop

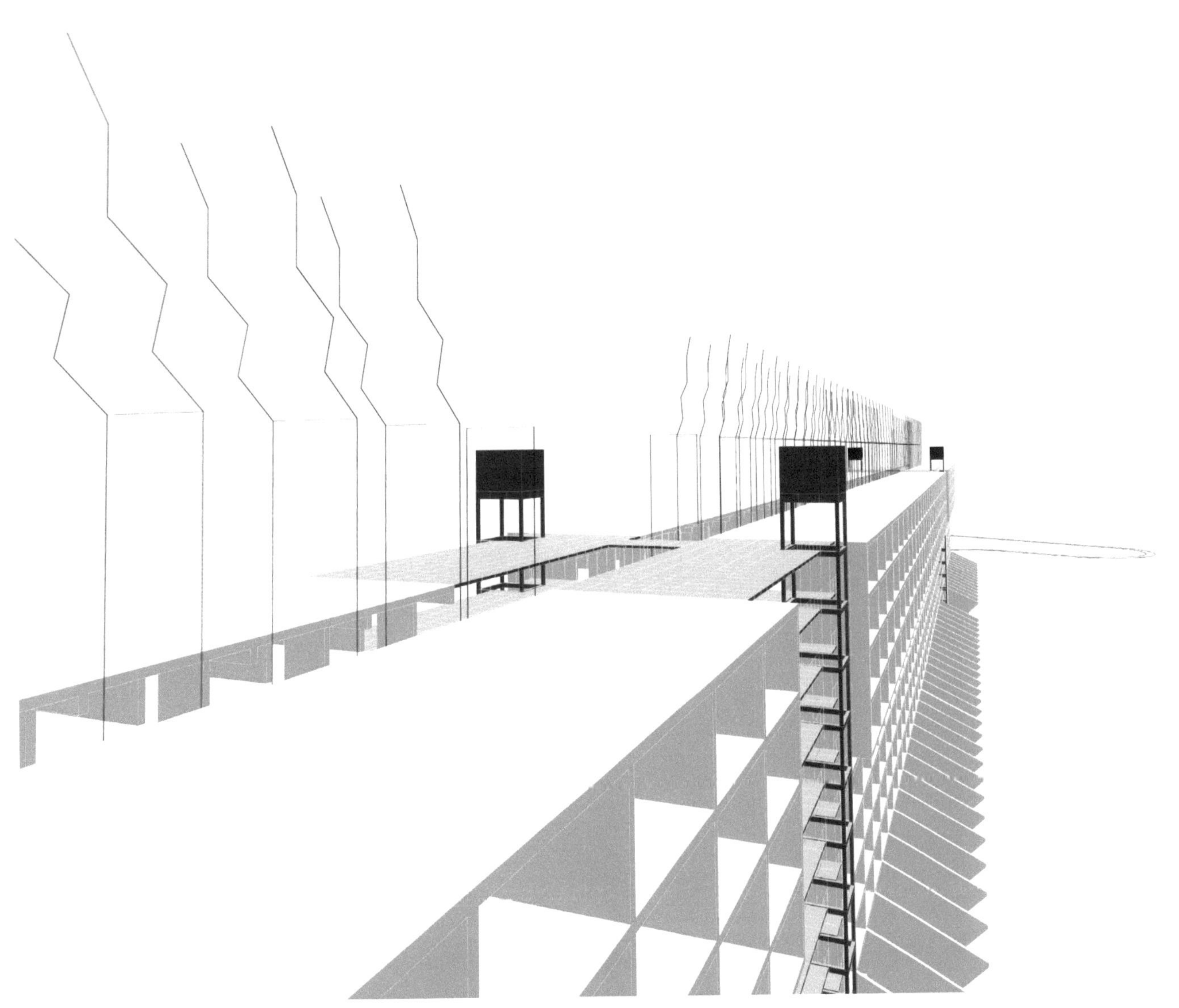

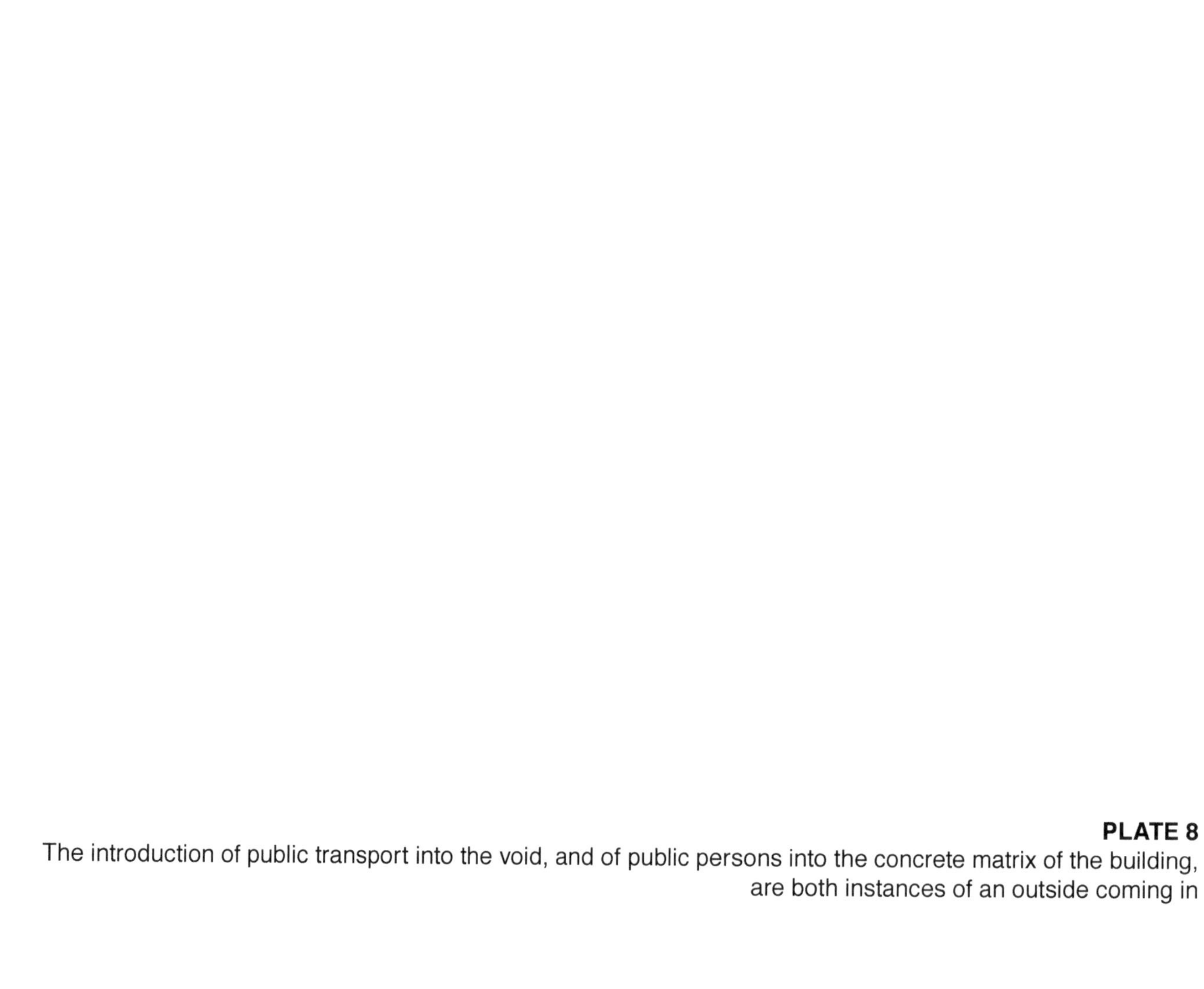

PLATE 8
The introduction of public transport into the void, and of public persons into the concrete matrix of the building, are both instances of an outside coming in

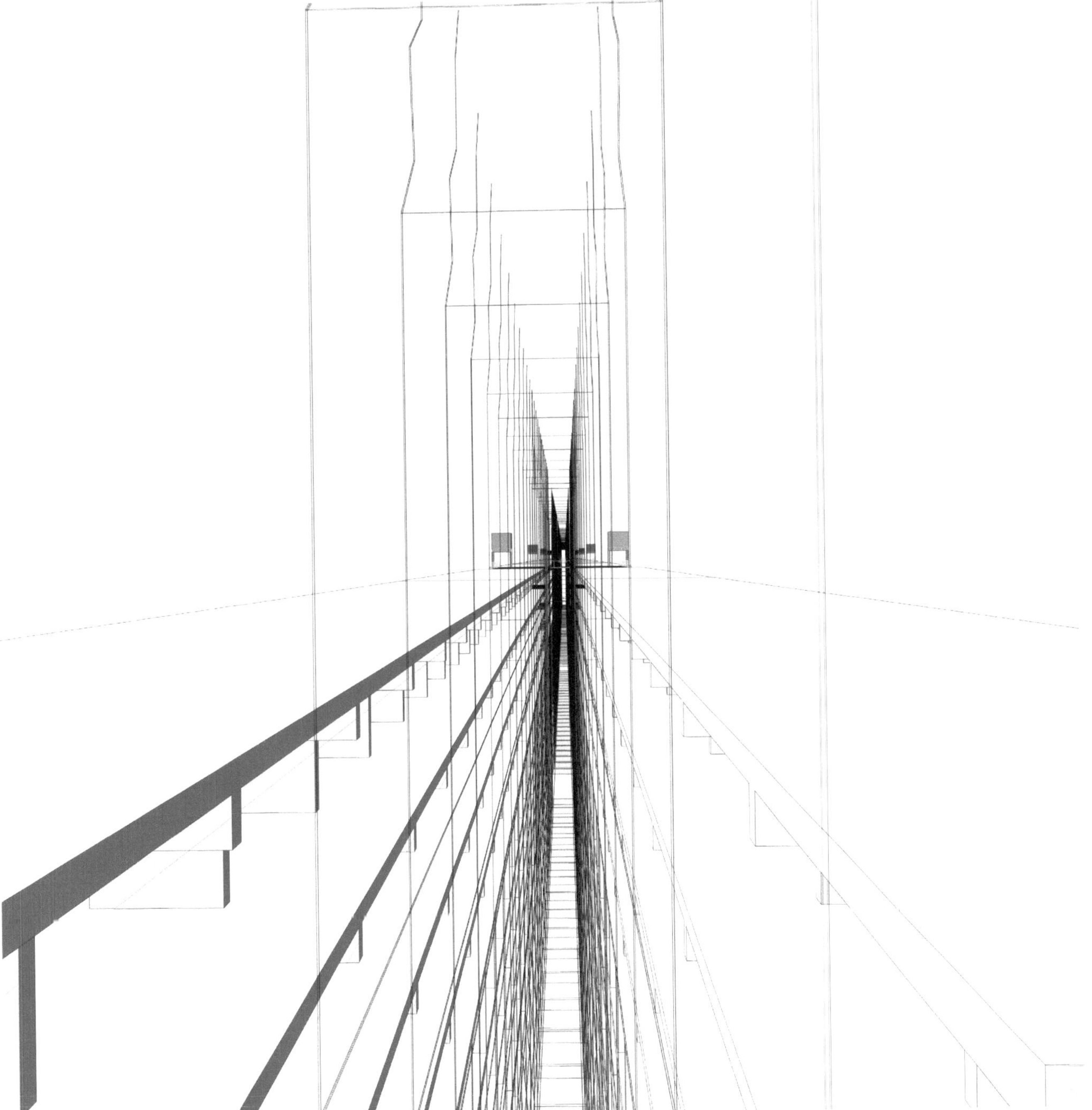

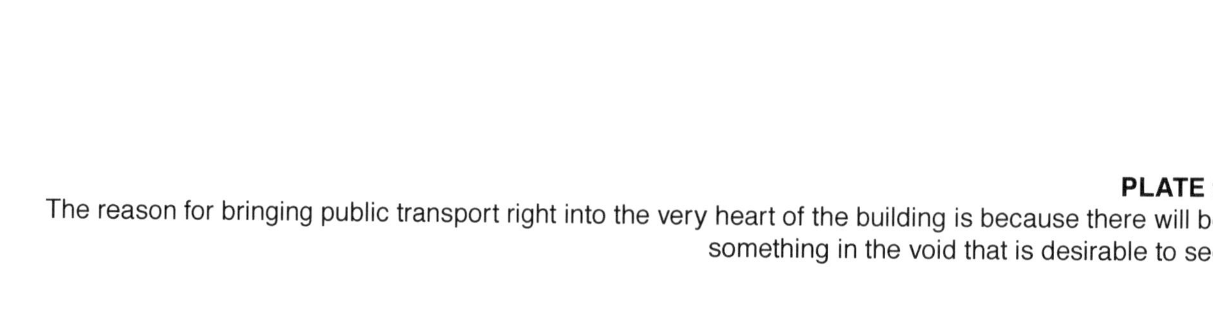

PLATE 9
The reason for bringing public transport right into the very heart of the building is because there will be something in the void that is desirable to see

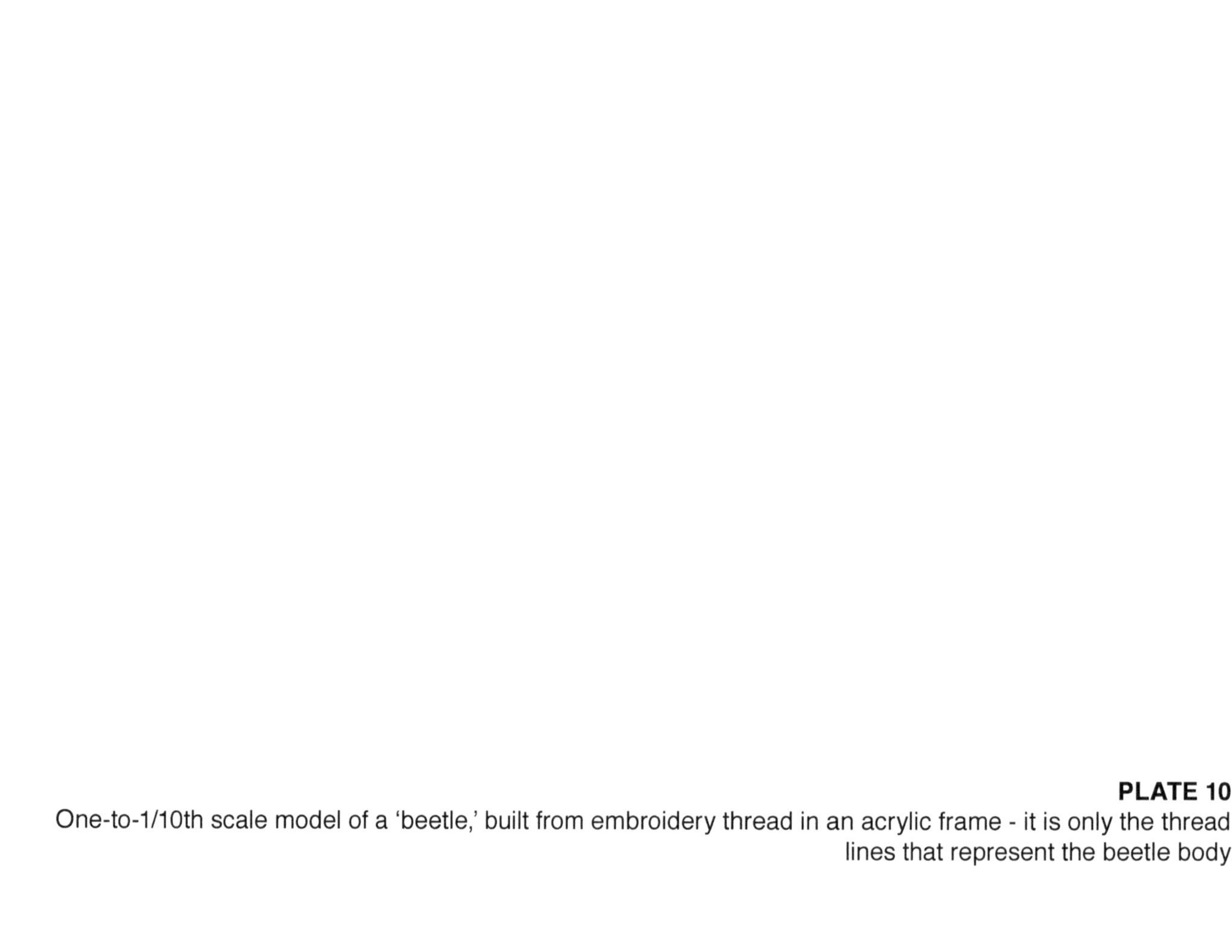

PLATE 10
One-to-1/10th scale model of a ‘beetle,’ built from embroidery thread in an acrylic frame - it is only the thread lines that represent the beetle body

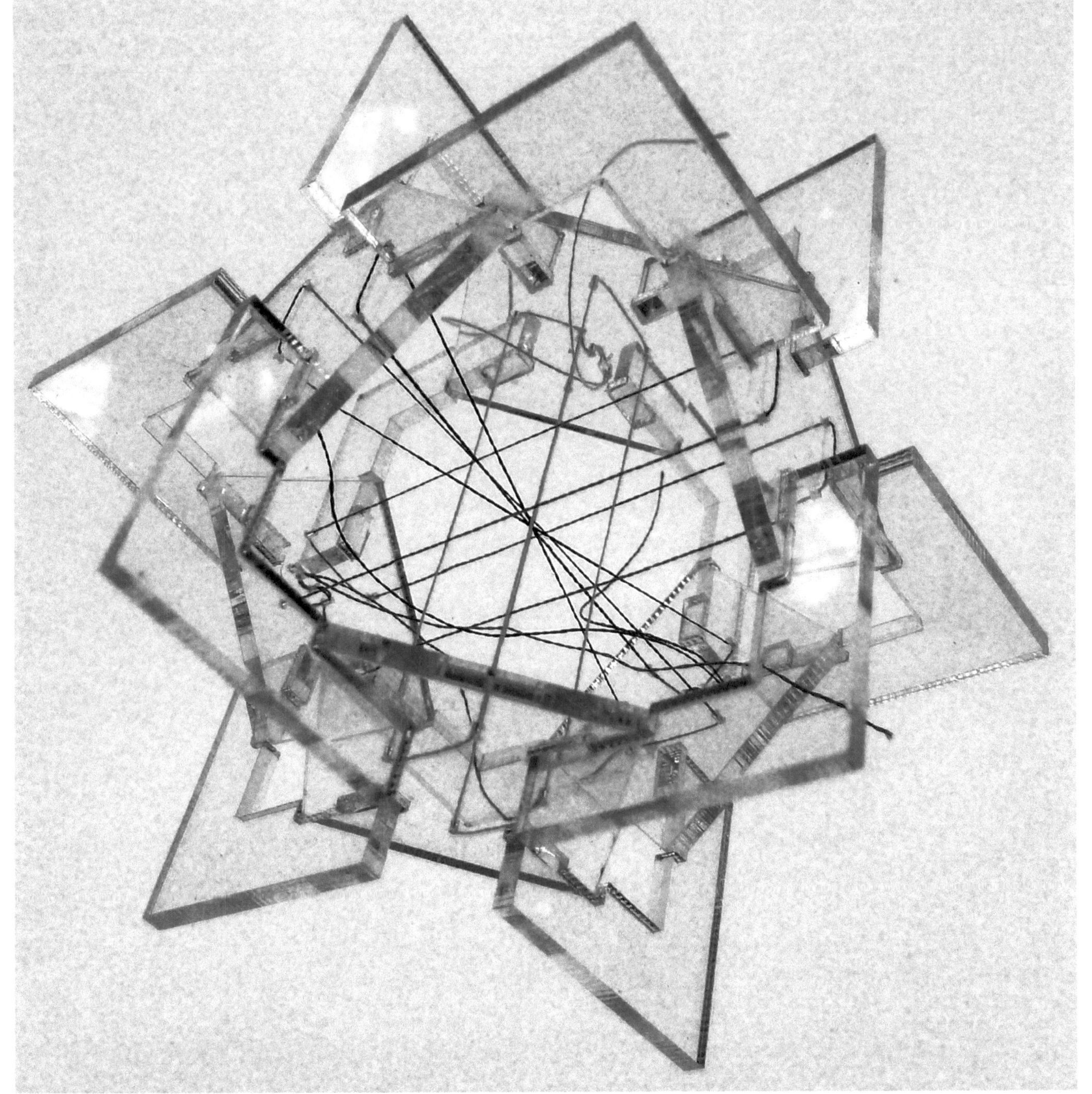

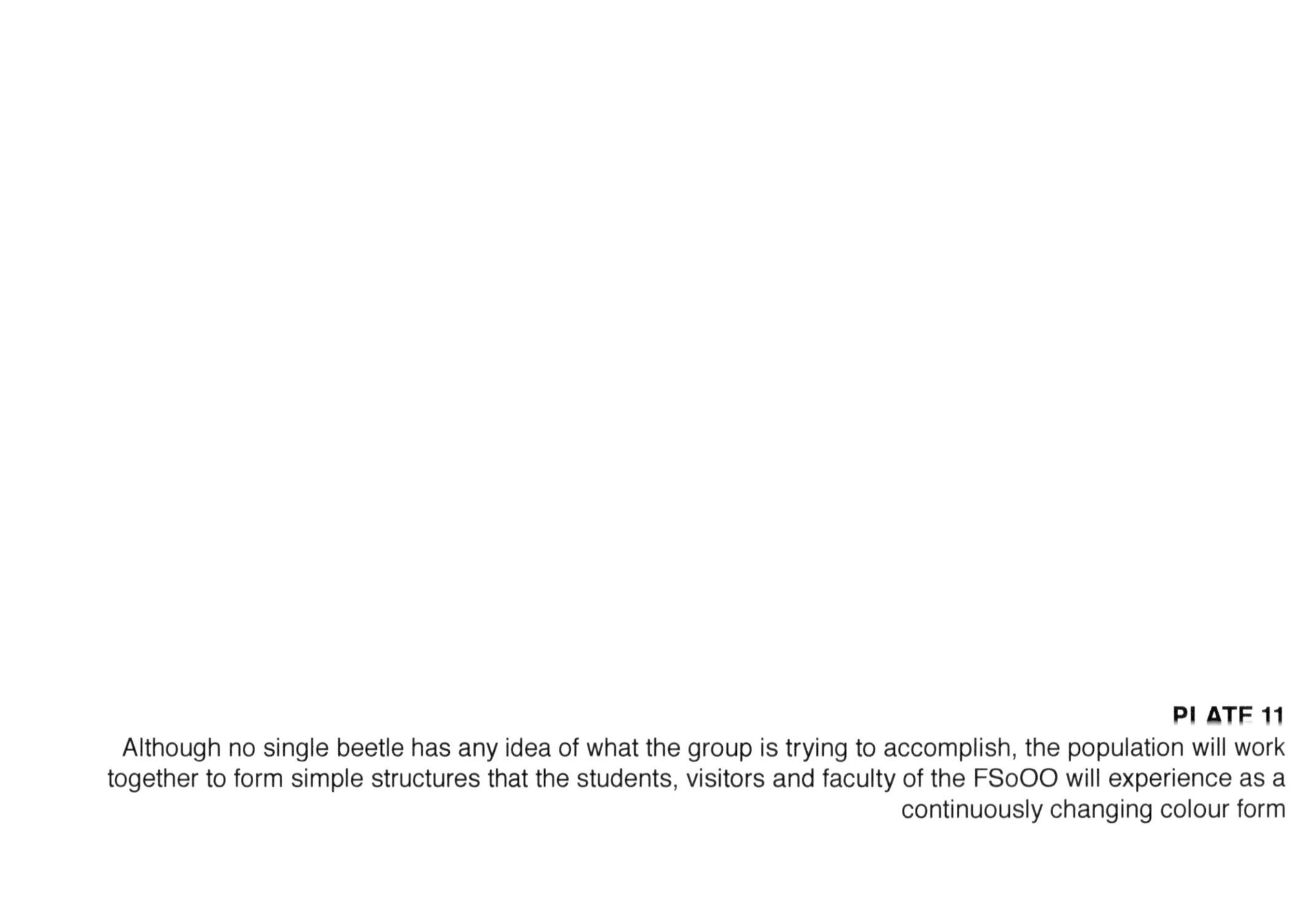

PLATE 11

Although no single beetle has any idea of what the group is trying to accomplish, the population will work together to form simple structures that the students, visitors and faculty of the FSoOO will experience as a continuously changing colour form

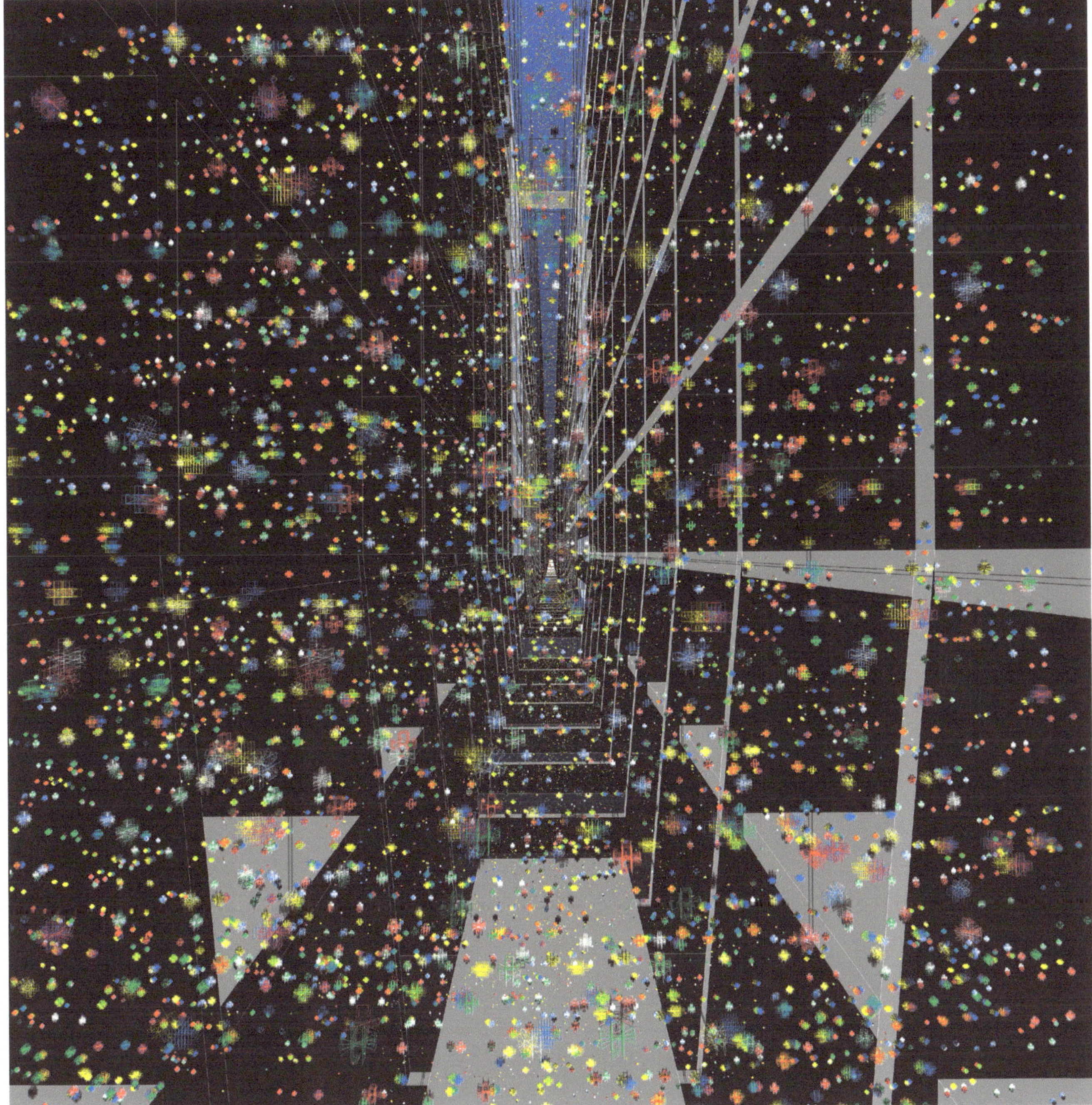

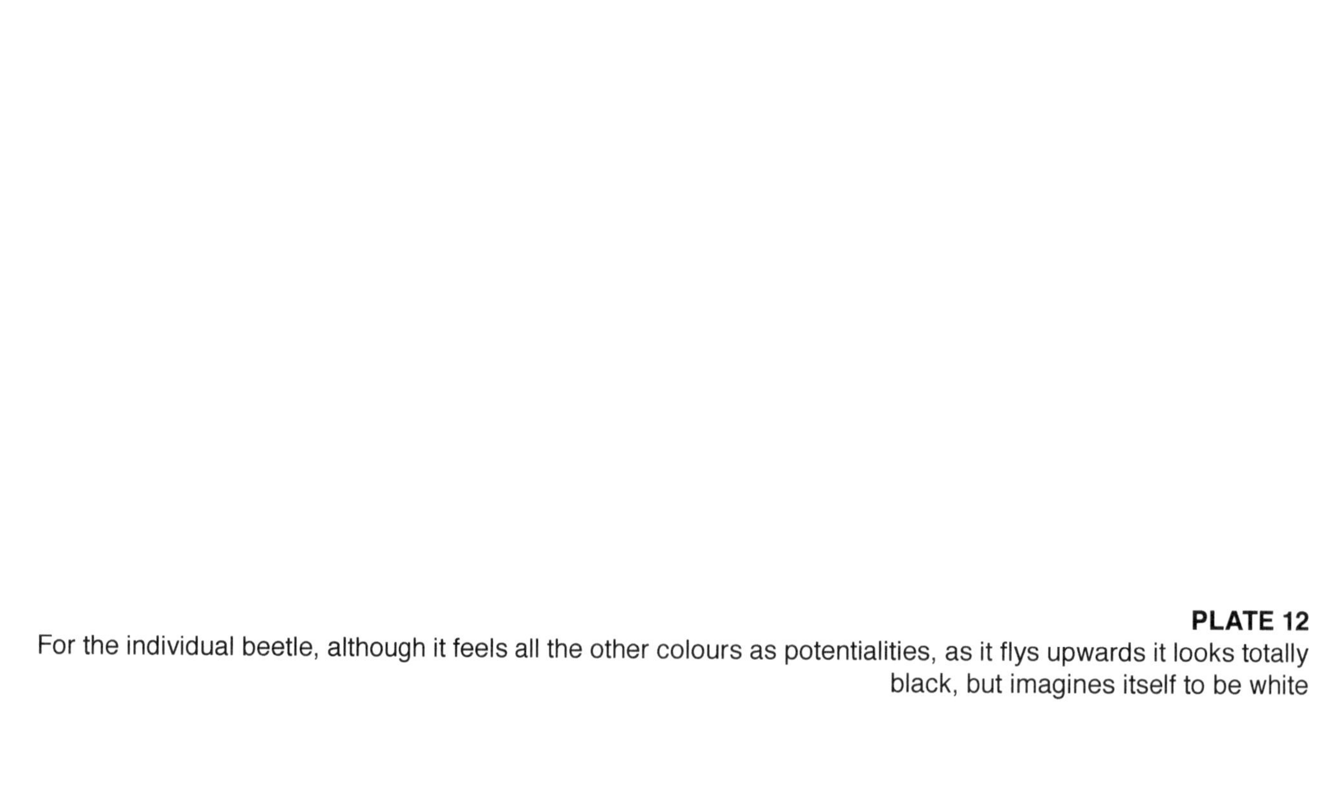

PLATE 12
For the individual beetle, although it feels all the other colours as potentialities, as it flys upwards it looks totally black, but imagines itself to be white

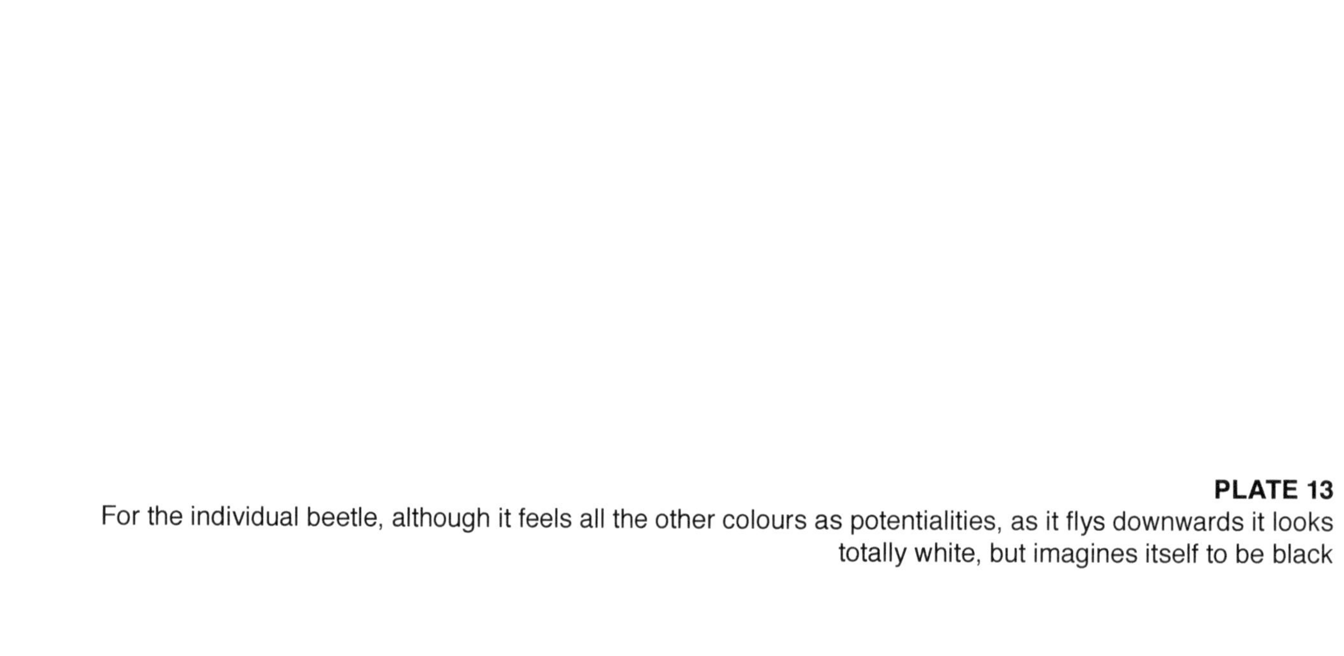

PLATE 13

For the individual beetle, although it feels all the other colours as potentialities, as it flys downwards it looks totally white, but imagines itself to be black

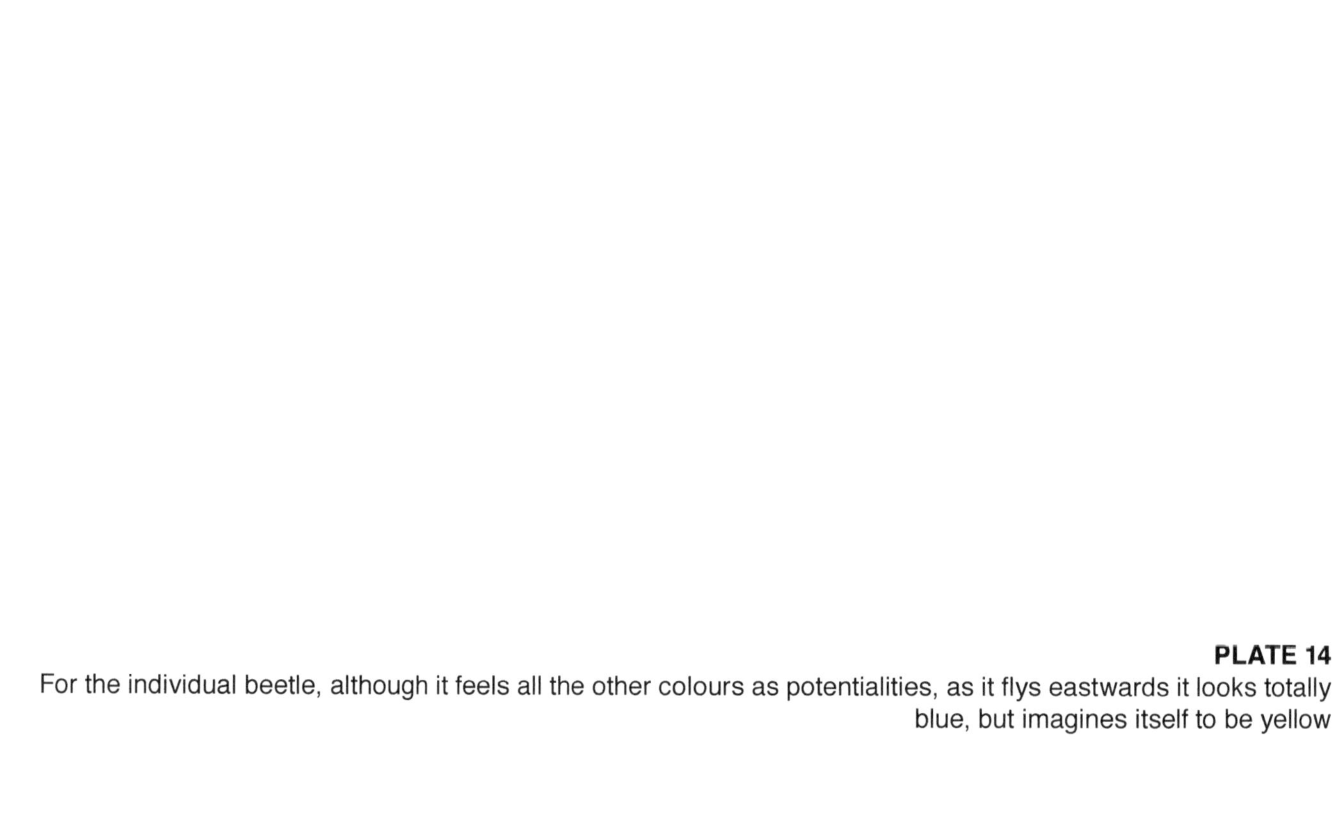

PLATE 14
For the individual beetle, although it feels all the other colours as potentialities, as it flys eastwards it looks totally blue, but imagines itself to be yellow

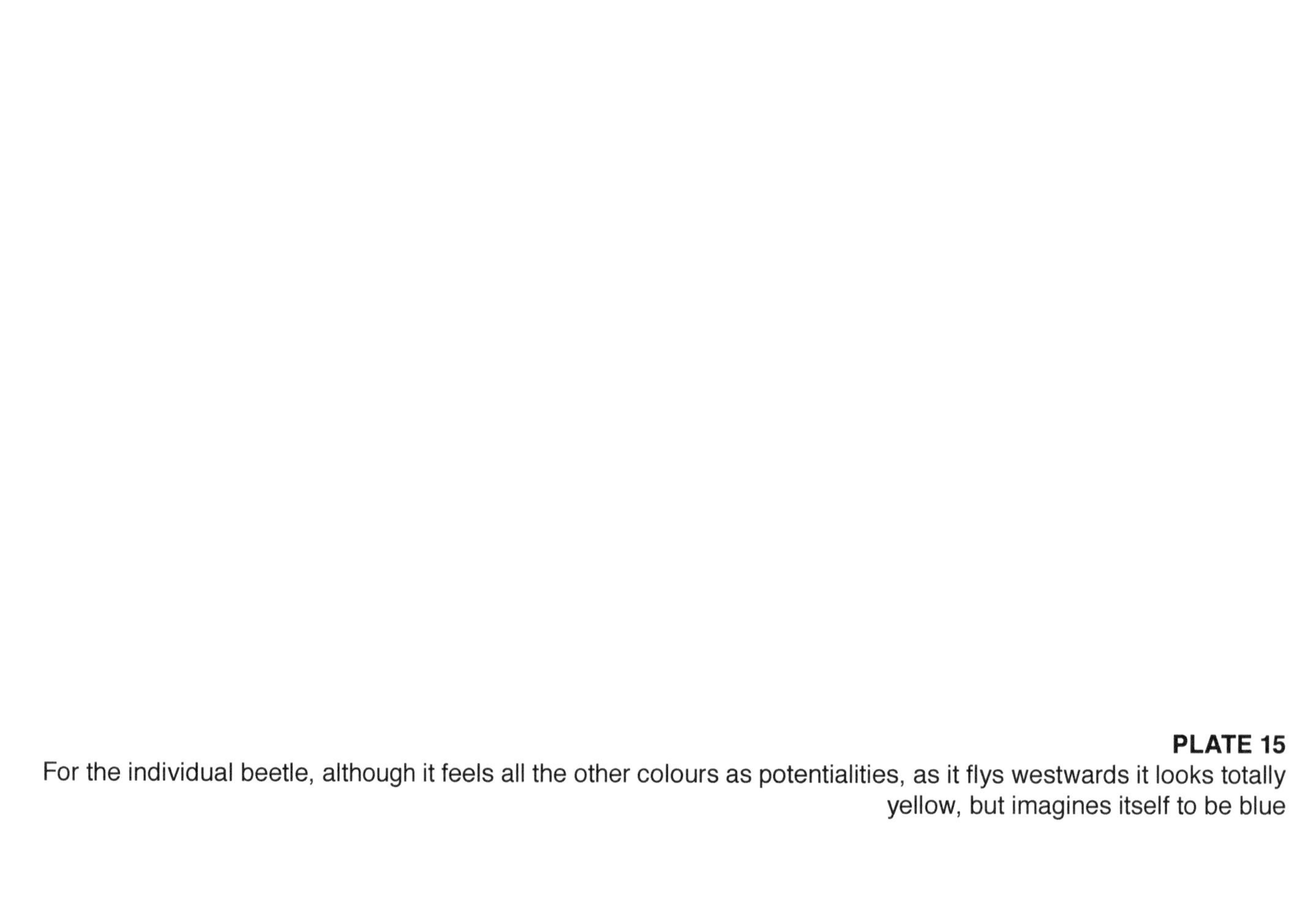

PLATE 15

For the individual beetle, although it feels all the other colours as potentialities, as it flys westwards it looks totally yellow, but imagines itself to be blue

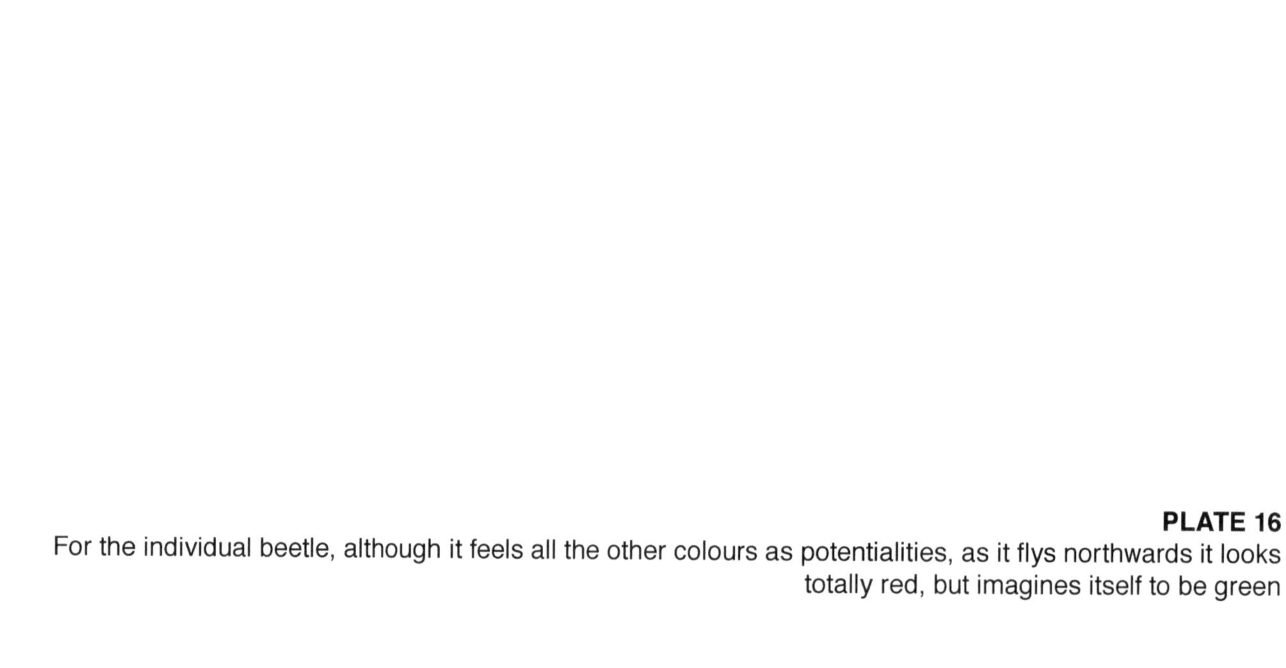

PLATE 16

For the individual beetle, although it feels all the other colours as potentialities, as it flys northwards it looks totally red, but imagines itself to be green

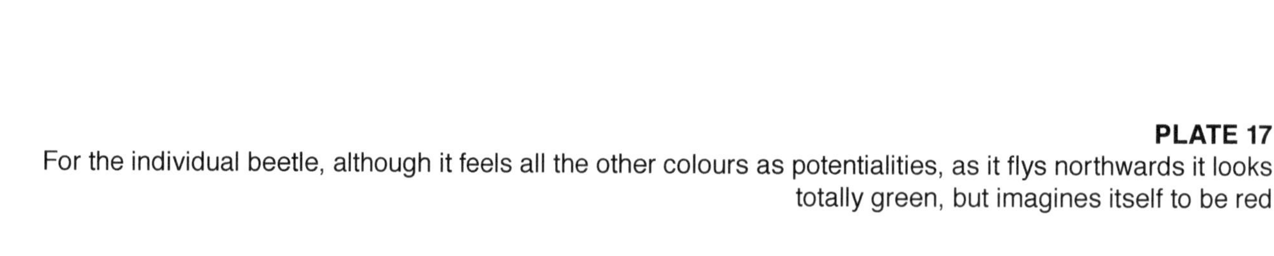

PLATE 17

For the individual beetle, although it feels all the other colours as potentialities, as it flys northwards it looks totally green, but imagines itself to be red

PLATE 18
Directed attention, series A.

PLATE 19
Directed attention, series B.

PLATE 20
Directed attention, series C.

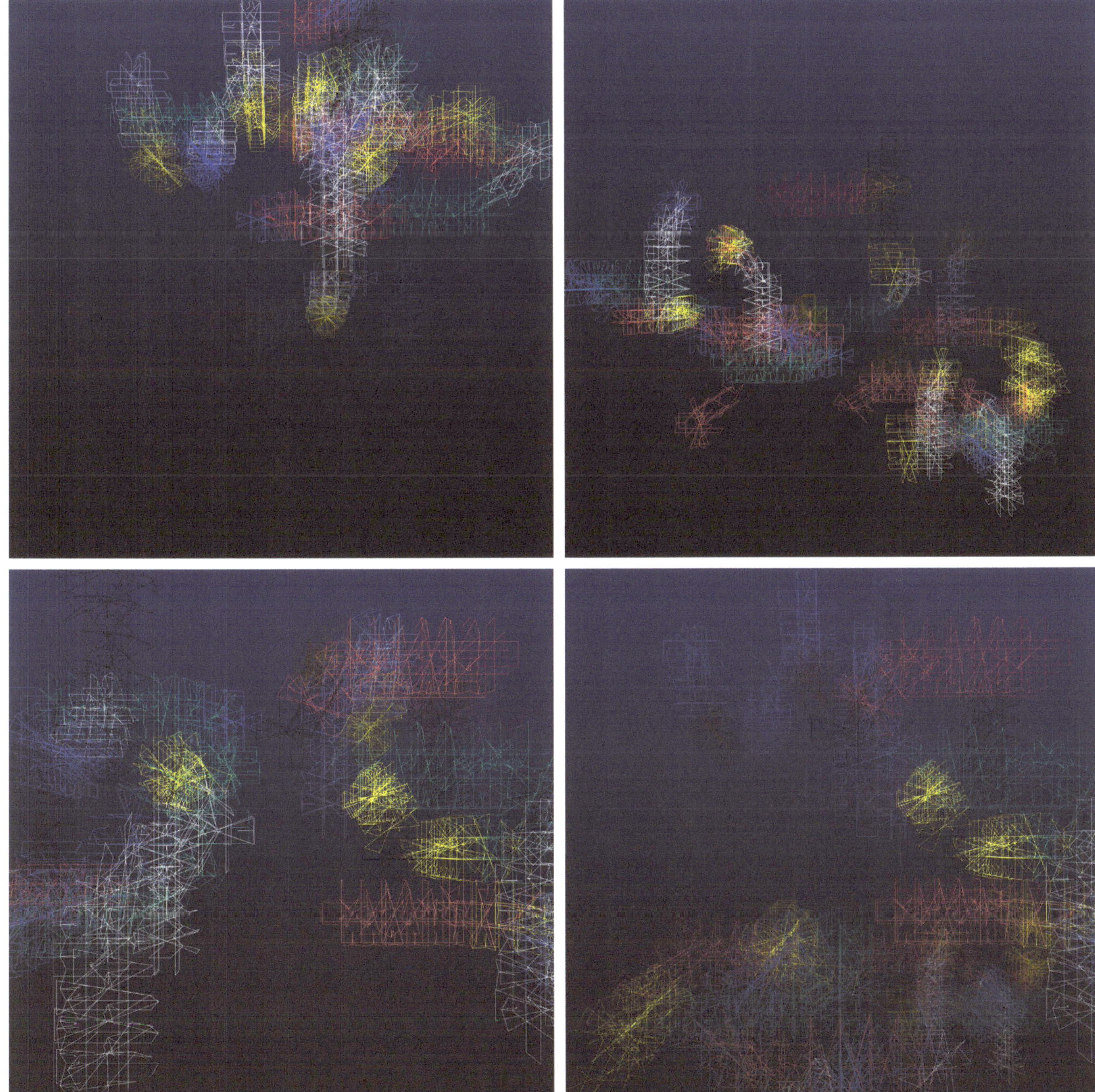

Notes

1. Manfredo Tafuri, *Architecture and Utopia, Design and Capitalist Development*, Barbara, Luigia La Penta (trans.), The MIT Press, Cambridge, Massachusetts, London, England, 1976, ix
2. Manfredo Tafuri, 'Wicked Architect,' *The Sphere and the Labyrinth, Avant-Gardes and Architecture from Piranesi to the 1970's*, Pellegrino d'Acierno and Robert Connolly (trans.), The MIT Press, Cambridge, Massachusetts, London, England, 1987, 29
3. See, Luigi Ficacci, Instituto Nazionale per la Grafica, Roma, *Giovanni Battista Piranesi, The Complete Etchings*, Taschen, Köln, London, Madrid, New York, Tokyo, 2000, 54-67
4. Ibid, 54
5. Translated in, Manfredo Tafuri, 'Wicked Architect,' 1987, 28
6. Ibid, 29
7. Ficacci, *Piranesi, Complete Etchings*, 2000, 394-431
8. Manfredo Tafuri, 'Wicked Architect,' 1987, 34
9. Ibid, 35
10. Ibid, 37
11. This is true whether the urban structure to be replaced is imagined as that of Piranesi's day, which he himself had helped to record in the Noli Plan of Rome; or if it is imagined to be that of the present day.
12. Piero Ostilio Rossi, *Roma, Guida all' architettura moderna, 1909-1991*, Editori Laterza, 1991, 321-323.
13. See, Berlage Institute,'The Postwar Asse Attrezzato,' *Rome The Centre(s) Elsewhere*, Berlage Institue, Rotterdam, Skira editore, Milan, 2010, 44-49
14. The group included Ludovico Quaroni, Bruno Zevi, Mario Fiorentino, Lucio & Vincenzo Passarelli, Ricardo Morandi and Gabriele Scimemi, see Manfredo Tafuri, History of Italian Architecture, 1944-1985, Jessica Levine (trans.), MIT Press, Cambridge Massachusetts; London, England, 1989, 82
15. 'On the ruins of XX century Rome,' L'architettura, Cronache e Storia, 238-39, august-september, 1975, 193
16. Ibid, 199
17. Ibid
18. See, for example, Benedetto Todaro, 'Corviale: Back to the Future, City of the living-city of the dead' and Enrico Puccini, 'Intervention idea for body structure 1, Typological revolution,' *Metamorfosi, quaderni di Architectura, 67,* July/August 2007, 26-31; 32-35
19. See, Nikos Salingaros, 'Tear Down the Corviale! New Urbanism Comes to Rome,' *Planetizen, Monday, May 24, 2010, http://www.planetizen.com/node/44338*
20. The authors of these projects are listed in, *Berlage Institute, Rome The Centre(s) Elsewhere*, 2010, 63-127.
21 Project by Ioanna Volaki, Berlage Institute, *Rome The Centre(s) Elsewhere*, 2010, 96-103.
22. See footnote 16
23. '*The real earth, viewed from above, is supposed to look like one of these balls made of twelve pieces of skin, variegated and marked out in various colours, of which the ones we know are only limited examples, like the paints which artists use, but there the whole earth is made up of such colours, and others far brighter and purer still. One section is a marvellously beautiful purple, and another is golden. All that is white of it is whiter than chalk or snow, and the rest is similarly made up of the other colours, still more and lovelier than those which we have seen. Even these very hollows in the*

earth, full of water and air, assume a kind of colour as they gleam amid the different hues around them, so that there appears to be one continuous surface of varied colours. The trees and flowers and fruits which grow upon this earth are proportionately beautiful. The mountains too and the stones have a proportionate smoothness and transparency, and their colours are lovelier.' Plato, Phaedo, 110 b-d

24. See footnote 16

25. It is beyond the scope of this paper to delve into scientific theories of human colour vision, for a good outline see, C.L. Hardin, 'Color Perception and Science,' *Colour for Philosophers, unweaving the rainbow,* Hackett Publishing Company, Indianapolis/Cambridge, 1988, 1-58.

Bibliography

Françoise Choay, *The Rule and the Model, On the Theory of Architecture and Urbanism*, The MIT Press, Cambridge Massachusetts, London, England, 1997

Luigi Ficacci, Instituto Nazionale per la Grafica, Roma, *Giovanni Battista Piranesi, The Complete Etchings*, Taschen, Köln, London, Madrid, New York, Tokyo, 2000

C.L. Hardin, *Colour for Philosophers, unweaving the rainbow*, Hackett Publishing Company, Indianapolis/ Cambridge, 1988,

Fredric Jameson, *Archaeologies of the Future, The Desire Called Utopia and Other Science Fictions*, Verso, London, New York, 2005

Jussu Parikka, *Insect Media, an archaeology of animals & technology*, University of Minnesota Press, Minneapolis, London, 2010

Giovanni Battista Piranesi, *Observations on the Letter of Monsieur Mariette; with Opinions on Architecture, and a Preface to a New Treatise on the Introduction and Progress of the Fine Arts in Ancient Times,* Caroline Beamish & David Britt, (trans.), Getty Research Institute, Los Angeles, 2002

Manfredo Tafuri, *Architecture and Utopia, Design and Capitalist Development*, Barbara, Luigia La Penta (trans.), The MIT Press, Cambridge, Massachusetts, London, England
Manfredo Tafuri, *1970's*, Pellegrino d'Acierno and Robert Connolly (trans.), The MIT Press, Cambridge, Massachusetts, London, England

Manfredo Tafuri, *History of Italian Architecture, 1944-1985*, Jessica Levine (trans.), The MIT Press, Cambridge Massachusetts, London, England, 1989

Manfredo Tafuri & Francesco Dal Co, *Modern Architecture/ 1&2,* Faber & Faber/Electa, London & Milan, 1976

Evan Thompson, *Colour Vision, a study in cognitive science and the philosophy of perception*, Routledge, London & New York, 1995

www.ingramcontent.com/pod-product-compliance
Ingram Content Group UK Ltd.
Pitfield, Milton Keynes, MK11 3LW, UK
UKHW060101300726
14090UKWH00003B/334

9780992876883